Grow Your Business

with **Google**

AdWords™

7 Quick and
Easy Secrets
for Reaching
More Customers
with the World's
#1 Search Engine

Grow Your Business with **Google AdWords**™

7 Quick and Easy Secrets for Reaching More Customers with the World's #1 Search Engine

Jon Smith

Mc
Graw
Hill

New York   Chicago   San Francisco   Lisbon   London
Madrid   Mexico City   Milan   New Delhi   San Juan
Seoul   Singapore   Sydney   Toronto

The *McGraw·Hill* Companies

1 2 3 4 5 6 7 8 9 0 DOC/DOC 0 1 0 9

ISBN 978-0-07-162959-1
MHID   0-07-162959-9

McGraw-Hill books are available at special quantity discounts to use as premiums and sales promotions, or for use in corporate training programs. To contact a representative please e-mail us at bulksales@mcgraw-hill.com.

This book is printed on recycled, acid-free paper.

Library of Congress Cataloging-in-Publication Data
Smith, Jon, 1975-

  Grow your business with Google Adwords : 7 quick and easy secrets for reaching more customers with the world's #1 search engine / by Jon Smith.
    p. cm.
  Includes index.
  ISBN 0-07-162959-9 (alk. paper)
  1. Google AdWords. 2. Google. 3. Internet marketing. 4. Internet advertising. I. Title.
  HF5415.1265.S6145 2010
  659.14'4—dc22   2009011283

Jo, thank you ;)

Contents

Introduction

Google is massive not just in terms of the company's fiscal wealth but also in terms of its power and influence on the Web. It is the most searched engine in the Western world and is not doing too badly everywhere else on the planet either.

You know something's big when a company name becomes a verb. I "google" job candidates before the interview, and many of my readers "google" me to check whether what I say works. Google *is* search. It is now so influential that if you've got an online business and want it to succeed, you simply have to sit up and pay attention.

This book is intended for Web site owners, marketing managers, project managers, and anyone interested in promoting a Web site effectively. It is also for non-

techies who want to be involved; it will show you how to research, prepare, and run your own AdWords campaign as well as give you the tools and the confidence to explain to other team members, third-party suppliers, and anyone else you care to talk to what it is you want them to do for you.

In *Be #1 on Google*, I explained to readers about the importance of improving a Web site's natural, or organic, listing and explored 52 proven techniques for rising up in the rankings. The techniques work, but with the best will in the world they don't happen overnight: It took me a few years of patience and constant tweaking to get the number 1 spot for the keyword "Jon Smith." The Web is evolving constantly: New Web sites pop up, and old ones drop off. As marketing professionals, we understand the importance of brand awareness, exposure, and "getting our name known and out there"—and that's where Google AdWords can come in. Remember, though, that Google AdWords is not a replacement for investing in optimizing your site; it should work hand in hand with your search engine optimization strategy.

An effective Google AdWords campaign is a necessity if you take your business seriously and want everybody else to as well. First, AdWords gives you a chance to build brand awareness cheaply and effectively. Your short- to medium-term plan may be to improve your natural listing on Google and other search engines, but you don't want to be sitting idly while this process is taking place—AdWords puts you in the search public's eye here and now. If your campaign is well thought out and well managed and you follow the advice in this book, you're going to be paying only when real prospects click through to a specific page, product, or area of your site—and there's a high probability that they are going to convert into customers. Second, AdWords can give you a real chance of getting big—fast. This isn't about just throwing a limitless budget at Google and seeing what happens with your fingers crossed, hoping that something will stick; quite simply, through a systematic and prepared campaign, you can grow fairly easily from obscurity to being a perceived market leader in less than six months—now how's that for a great return on investment?

AdWords is a new breed of online advertising that adheres to the fundamental rules of marketing, but with its own unique twist—Google won't reveal what works and what doesn't because that would lead to users abusing the system, so it keeps quiet. There is no official users' manual to Google AdWords, but I trust you will find this "unofficial" guide clear, concise, and effective. I've tested these techniques on a number of sites, some high-profile and some more obscure, and I assure you they work—and work well.

Ready to get started? Then let me take your hand (metaphorically speaking, of course). . . .

Grow Your Business with **Google** AdWords™

7 Quick and Easy Secrets for Reaching More Customers with the World's #1 Search Engine

1

AdWords—What's It All About?

In the Beginning . . .

My professional online marketing career began in 1998. Although the Internet as a medium for exchanging information already was established, certainly among techies and academics, the whole concept of e-commerce and the marketing machine that would go behind promoting and monetizing online businesses was still very much in its infancy.

As a team of about 30 individuals, we were about to unleash Amazon.co.uk onto the British public. Not only were we trying to build brand awareness of a new business, we were trying to do it through a medium most of our potential customers were unaware of and, worse, afraid of! We not only had to educate people about our new exciting bookstore, we had to assure them that online ordering was safe, secure, and reliable. All things considered, we did a pretty good job, but it's fair to say that many of our efforts were hit and miss, and a lot could be attributed to luck—being in the right place at the right time and taking a few risks that really paid off.

Online marketing was new, online marketing was an unknown, but mainly . . . online marketing was a mess. Advertisers had no idea how much to pay and how best to track performance, and the portals and high-traffic sites offering advertising space had no real idea how much their space was worth. Some incredible amounts of money changed hands over the following years, and then, as is well documented, the entire Internet industry was forced to face up to the realities of economics. The dot-com bubble burst—billions of pounds and dollars were simply gone. There were a few survivors, Amazon being one of them, but there were lots and lots of casualties, some of them high-profile but also many that hadn't even enjoyed a few months of paper success.

Online marketing and advertising didn't cause the dot-com boom, but it did play a part in the superhigh valuations being placed on dot-com companies at the time. When the shaky foundations of overvalued and poorly planned multi-billion-dollar companies gave way, it all came tumbling down.

The truth was out: To make an online business successful, you still needed to adhere to the basic rules of good old-fashioned bricks and mortar businesses. That realization forced a rethinking of how to market Web sites. Advertisers no longer were prepared to just outbid their rivals and throw piles of cash away on banner ads, skyscrapers, and rotating animated GIFs (Graphic Interface Formats)—online advertising had to get clever. Advertising and marketing in general needed to follow the same rules as their offline cousin—ROI (return on investment). The hedonistic days of paying a flat fee or rental for a prime "real estate" position for your banner ad had gone, as had the short-lived fad of *cost per thousand,* or paying a site every time it served your advertisement to a thousand visitors, whether or not the ad resulted in an attributable sale.

It all changed when Google came along with AdWords. In fairness, when it was launched in 2002, AdWords was a bit on the low-quality side and was really just a rehash of what organizations such as Overture were trying to do at the time. However, Google did it slicker and smarter. Google listened to what its users (read: advertisers; read: paymasters) wanted and implemented those ideas. Google quickly became the market leader in paid-for placement, or *search advertising,* and no one has knocked the company off its perch yet.

How important is Google AdWords to your business? Very important. In fact, I'll go so far as to say that you are not utilizing the potential of your online business fully *unless* you are using Google AdWords.

You've Changed Your Tune—What about Organic Listings?

In *Be #1 on Google*, Google AdWords is barely mentioned—and with good reason; the book's aim is to focus your efforts on optimizing your site so that it is easily found and highly ranked within the natural or organic search results of Google and other search engines. But that's not to say that AdWords wasn't important then (and now)—far from it! Search Engine Optimization (SEO) and search advertising are two different beasts and work completely independently of each other. You can have a strong SEO campaign and a weak AdWords campaign or vice versa, but what's going to get potential consumers clicking on links, visiting your site, and becoming customers of your services or products? When you have a strong presence in both, customers need to be able to find you by natural search *and* by search advertising—it's their choice, it's their Web session, and it's *your* job to ensure that your Web site is there no matter what route users take. This book focuses on Google AdWords, so you'll need to put your hand in your pocket again and buy *Be #1 on Google* if you're looking for SEO advice.

Yes, but If You Had to Choose One, Would It Be Google Organic or Google AdWords?

They're different! Stop comparing them. Here's my philosophy on this. I'm a strong believer in making the Web sites I'm involved with easy to find. That means optimizing the pages so that they can rank highly in natural search *and* in paid search advertising. First, the way I look at it, it's better to take up two (or more) of the slots available on page 1 of the search results than one—and that means paying for at least one of those listings through AdWords. Second, SEO is not an exact science. Google and the other search engines are forever modifying their algorithms to keep Web site owners guessing: Just as you achieve the exalted number 1 slot for your favorite keyword, it all changes and you find yourself banished to the depths of page 15, and then it all starts again. Because no money changes hands, you're not in control and cannot shout at anyone when things go wrong. With Google AdWords, you get what you pay for. It's the act of paying for this service that means that there *is* a science to it. There has to be; otherwise, put simply, if it wasn't working for companies (and working effectively), they would stop using the service. Is Google seeing a rise or fall in take-up and expenditure on its AdWords program? Well, you've just bought this book. What do you think?

Google's Intent

If you still need convincing about whether you can go it solo by just banking on your current search results ranking without the added benefit and safety net of AdWords, think about this: Google's success is due in part to its refreshingly sparse look and feel. This "clutter-free" approach was and still is an oasis of calm in what is a very busy online landscape. Google is a search engine, and its main feature—nay, its *raison d'être*—is the search box, with cursor flashing, awaiting your query. Google has never sold space on its home page to advertisers. Advertising and commercial promotion are not Google's focus; information is. Google offers as many tools and applications as, if not more than, any of the leading portal sites, yet the home page is pretty much as bare as it was way back in 1998—the aim then and now is to offer users an effective search engine.

Where the large portals of the late 1990s and early 2000s went wrong was in cramming the home page with links to every service and feature and confusing that with excessive amounts of third-party advertising. Why? Because that was how they made money. Google's primary job, if you like, is to return accurate responses to user queries—the priority is to provide users with information about the word or phrase queried. By nature, this means that Web sites that provide information will always rank higher than will profit-driven sites (i.e., commercial or e-commerce sites). Although there are techniques you can employ to buck the trend, you will always be playing second fiddle to informational sites. Therefore, if you truly accept what Google's main purpose is, it doesn't take a quantum leap to realize that since there is a paid-for search advertising facility available through Google, you can rest assured that it's there for a reason. Yes, of course, Google is a business and wants to make money, but it can do that through AdWords while ensuring that users come back again and again because Google Search works so well. Google's purpose is to offer users unbiased answers to their queries. Its algorithm (despite constantly changing) will always prefer an informational Web site to a commercial one. Therefore, if you've got something to sell, Google is basically insisting that you pay to advertise your site, and in return Google will send you interested, relevant, and "targeted" users who have a genuine interest in your product or service. You pay; they deliver.

No Inbound Links, No Joy . . .

A critical component of SEO has always been links. A few years ago this caused a craze, with every Web owner flooding its site with links to other Web sites in return for reciprocal links from those other Web sites. Web owners abused the system, and Google was forced to make some changes. The zeitgeist now is to favor *inbound links*—lots of other Web sites linking to you, thus giving you "authority" status in the eyes of Google as long as you do not reciprocate those links. A site that has lots of inbound links tends to enjoy a very high ranking on Google Search. Thus, it could be argued that the key to SEO is thousands of inbound links . . . and herein lies the problem. Who is going to want to link to you? If your pages are content-rich, unbiased, informational, and informative, you stand a fighting chance, but you're looking at promoting your Web site through AdWords because you run a business—and therefore your Web site is commercial by definition. Yes, I'm sure you've got great copy, great product or service descriptions, and great images and your sales messages are world-beating, but you'll never be "content-rich" in the true sense and therefore very few Web sites are going to want to link to you. Enter AdWords, the great leveler. With AdWords, it doesn't matter if you don't have any inbound links or whether Google sees your site as authoritative—if you get your campaign right, you'll be displayed on page 1 every time.

When's a Good Time to Start an AdWords Campaign?

Now! Seriously, if your site is live, it's time to start your campaign as soon as possible; you need to be using AdWords immediately (although, obviously, you should give this book a quick once-over first). Why the rush? Well, for starters, AdWords really works, and depending on your industry, it can work for you with a small to medium-size investment. The reason AdWords is so effective is that every aspect of your campaign is measurable, and in terms of cost per new customer, you'd be hard pressed to find anything else that works out to be so affordable and offers a global reach 24 hours a day, seven days a week. On top of that, the major reason you need to start your AdWords campaign *now* is that it still needs to catch on. Seriously, despite the fact that it is almost seven years old, a lot of companies have yet to (1) realize it's there and (2) realize its full potential. Believe it or not, you're still one of the early adopters, and if your budget is tight, you still can get an effective campaign operational for a very small outlay. Inevitably, this will all change when your competition decides to focus a bit more effort on search advertising—but before then, get big fast and blow them out of the water!

Controlling What Users See

AdWords puts you back in the driver's seat. You might have spent hours optimizing your pages, but that's no guarantee that Google will index each page as highly as you would like. Your Web site may not rank at all, or, worse, sometimes the wrong pages are ranking highly.

For the search term "*Monte Cristo Musical,*" I have positions 1, 2, 3, and 6 of the natural listings. I'm pretty pleased about that. However, the listing on position 3 quotes the Flash source file behind the site. It's not a huge problem, because the link takes users to the Web site I want them to visit, but Google is displaying some of the "code" behind the site:

```
[FLASH] <p align="left"><font face="Tahoma" size="10" color="#e5e1ba
...
File Format: Shockwave Flash
<font color="#ffffff"> </font></font></p> MONTE CRISTO by Jon Smith &
Leon Parris Running Time: 2:21 MONTE CRISTO - THE MUSICAL COMPLETED,
MAY 2007. ...
www.montecristothemusical.com/sources.swf - Similar pages - Note this
```

This is not the sales message I created, it is not the "look" I want for my listing, and it's highly unlikely that anyone would want to click through to find out more. Thankfully, this search result is sandwiched between search results that use the

<title> and <description> I wrote, and I still get the visitors. But what if this was my only search result? I wouldn't have visitors. This is where AdWords really helps: You can dictate the message, the positioning, how often the ad is served, to which locations, and, depending on your budget, how many people can both see and click through to your page—and it's your control over the destination page that is critical. If you're an online store selling teapots and speciality teas and want to promote your herbal range, you can do just that, bringing users right to where you want them rather than to your generic home page or, in the case above, to a page of Google's choosing!

You Stroke My Back . . .

This really is conjecture—and certainly when I asked Google customer support, they categorically denied it—but I believe that having a long campaign history with Google has benefits. It's quite simple, really: Google is a business and wants to encourage proven advertisers. If you have a history with Google and your campaigns have a good click-through rate, I can't help feeling that you are offered slightly cheaper bids for higher positions. I can't prove it because I haven't run exactly the same campaign from two different accounts.

Whether it's true or not, the sooner you're up and running (and spending money) with Google, the better. Yes, some of your competitors will always have a longer track record than yours—that's life. But if you open your first Google Ad-Words campaign today, you're still an early adopter in the grand scheme of things. Think of the many hundreds of thousands, if not millions, of advertisers who still have not used AdWords. You'll always have a longer campaign history than they do.

2

Defining Your Strategy

To harness the potential of Google AdWords fully, it's of paramount importance to understand fully what Google AdWords is, how it works, and how you can make it work for you and your online business. You may have dabbled with AdWords already and enjoyed some success or suffered abject failure. You may have been using AdWords for years and are reading this book to find a couple of hints and tips to improve your current campaigns. Whatever your background with AdWords is, it never hurts to take a breather, refresh yourself, and "go back to the basics"—not the least because Google is always changing and we all run the risk of falling into a rut with our behavior and thought processes, which means we often overlook some of the simple ways to improve our campaigns.

Google AdWords in a Nutshell

AdWords is advertising, pure and simple. Google knows it has a search engine that works and that users trust. Among the many millions of searches that take place on Google every single day, some of them will be for a word or phrase (*keyword*) that relates to the product or service your Web site offers. Users see the search results to that keyword query in list format, and from there they may or may not click on a link to a Web site. If you are lucky, there is a link to your Web site on page 1 of those search results, but for many of us that isn't the case. Although there is a lot that can be done in terms of Search Engine Optimization, this might take a while to come into effect, and if it's a particularly busy and competitive market, we might never see our site ranked on the first page. So what's a marketer to do? Give up?

No. AdWords gives you an opportunity to place an advertisement in front of Google users who are searching for one of your keywords, with immediate effect. Those users may be searching for that word or phrase for a host of reasons—not everyone is shopping 24/7, although as optimistic marketing types, we wish they were. There will be users who search for "Jimmy Choo shoes" but don't actually want to buy them, ever—e.g., me! I searched for them to find out what all the fuss was about, and to be honest, I still don't understand. But then, I'm a guy, and no matter how deeply in touch I am with my feminine side, I'll never wear heels or spend more than about a hundred dollars for a pair of shoes for me or anyone else! Multiply this scenario across the day and it's apparent that most users are searching primarily for information, not for a place to spend their hard-earned cash next. However, some of those users *are* looking to buy, and, even though you might have set up your Web site only this morning, you conceivably can be listed on page 1 of the search results tonight if that's what you want.

Let's say you've decided to retail garden gnomes. You've got a brand-new Web site, but with no track record, no brand awareness, and no links, you're not regarded as an authority. You've just received your first consignment of garden gnomes from a supplier in Malaysia, and you're ready to go. You write the first AdWords campaign in the morning, turn it on at lunchtime, and bang!—there you are, top of the pile on page 1 that afternoon. But what's really great about AdWords is that it's set up to cost you money only when it's working for you. All those users who are searching for images of garden gnomes just for something to do on a rainy day aren't costing you money—they'll see your ad, ignore it, and click on the link to a garden gnome fan site or something similar. For the users who *do* want to buy garden gnomes, the likelihood is that they're going to be more open to reading and processing sales messages. They're keen to buy, and your slickly written advertisement is just the right medicine. They click, it costs you cash, but then they've found your site and will, one hopes, go on to become one of your first customers (not bad considering that you turned on AdWords only a few hours ago).

AdWords works because it is so unobtrusive—obvious to those on the lookout for what it is you sell or do yet just part of the background for those who are intent on something else—and the best part is that you are paying for it only when it's working for you. Never before has an advertiser had so much control over where, when, and how an ad is displayed, and the depth and breadth of the data you can receive on an advertisement's effectiveness (or not, as the case may be) are staggering. Google AdWords is your friend.

Getting Results with Google AdWords—Abridged

There are, of course, exceptions to the rule and other factors that must be considered, which we'll explore throughout this book, but generally speaking, the more you are prepared to bid for a customer's click on your ad (in comparison to your competition), the higher up the list your ad appears. Other factors, of course, come into play, such as relevancy, but as a baseline AdWords is driven by how much you're prepared to pay Google per click and how much other advertisers are prepared to pay for the same keyword. Money talks. Now, the clever thing about AdWords is that Google does not value the depth of your wallet over all else. You see, your *ad rank* also is decided by how effective your ad is.

Now, assuming your ad is ranked somewhere within the top six, you'll begin, we hope, to receive *click-throughs*. The rate of click-throughs you receive in comparison to how many times the ad was shown (impressions) is represented as the click-through rate (CTR). This is expressed as a percentage figure. If your ad does not receive enough click-throughs (approximately one for every 200 impressions), Google will decrease how often it shows the ad. If the ad continues to fail, Google will disable it because it's not working for either of you.

I'm loath to say what a good CTR is or what CTR you should be aiming for, because it depends on so many factors, not the least of which is how much you're paying per click and, if that click-through results in a user buying a product or a service from you, how much you charge for your product or service and how much of that is profit. So I will leave you to decide for yourself what a good CTR is and what a good conversion rate is, because that is particular to your unique business.

The good news is that although you may have to bid high to get your new ad campaign established at first, if you have created an effective ad that attracts users and therefore results in click-throughs, Google will regard your ad well. Google rewards ads that work and will begin to lower the cost-per-click price of your ad—so each click will begin to cost you less while you continue to maintain your high position. The more successful your ad is, the cheaper each click-through becomes, and so you get more clicks for your money. Assuming these click-throughs convert into customers, you'll have even more money to spend on AdWords, and the cycle continues. If only everything worked as smoothly as this! Unfortunately, there will be other advertisers competing for the same keywords with similar ads, all looking to jostle you for your position. This makes AdWords a constantly changing landscape, and it is imperative that you keep your eye on the ball.

Now, as a high CTR is one of the determining factors in your ad's quality score and thus positioning (and therefore in the success of your ad campaign), it should be easy to see why writing that "killer" ad is paramount. It is the ad copy that will attract users to click on your ad; it is the ad copy that will make your ad stand out from the other ads listed for that keyword . . . and every ad starts with a headline. A poor headline—or, worse, a headline that becomes part of the generic "noise" on the page—is going to fail to attract clicks, and although nonclicks aren't costing you money, they're not making you money either.

Sadly, it's not as easy as creating a winning ad and then sitting back and counting your millions. Oh, no. You see, your competitors can see what your ad looks like, and if it's perceived to be more successful than theirs, they're going to modify and improve their ads. These competitor alterations will affect your CTR, and you'll need to modify and improve your ad to stay ahead of the game. You should know now that embarking on an AdWords campaign can help you reap rewards, but it is time-consuming and involves real work. If you're not prepared to work at it, it's probably best to stop before you start and put an ad in the Yellow Pages instead.

Still with me? Great. Let's explore some of this in a bit more detail. . . .

Setting Up Your "Campaign"

There's little point in repeating what is freely available within the extensive help and info pages available on the Google Web site. What I will do, though, is expand on the areas where new users seem to have problems when first trying to navigate their way around while setting up their first campaigns.

An important variable you will need to decide on at the campaign level is the *networks* on which your ads will be shown. The good news is that you can edit your choices at a later date, depending on whether you want to expand or reduce your exposure. These are the choices:

Google Search

This is pretty self-explanatory: the "Google Search" page. When a user enters a keyword or phrase into Google's Search box, Google displays the results on a "Search results" page. Now, on which Google search results page your ad will be displayed and in which position will be determined by the keywords you have chosen and the amount you have bid per click, plus a host of other determining factors that will be explained later.

Search Network

This is the generic term for Google's recognized partners. This list of partners will change over time, but they are trusted sites with which Google has a corporate relationship. Examples include AOL and Ask.com. So if you decide to advertise on the Search Network, chances are that your ads will be shown to users searching on partner Web sites other than Google. Bear in mind that although Google is big, 20 percent of Web searches are taking place on search engines other than Google. That's one in five searches. Displaying your ads on the Search Network is a simple way to expand your exposure to non-Google users without having to set up numerous ad campaigns with numerous separate search engines.

Content Network

The official info page from Google explains that the Content Network "comprises hundreds of thousands of high-quality websites, news pages and blogs that partner with Google to display targeted AdWords ads." The info page shows the branding of msnbc.com, nytimes.com, cspan.org, and neimanmarcus.com as example network partners. It is indeed true that there are a number of "authority" Web sites with good content and high traffic that are signed up as Content Network partners, but for every one of these recognizable Web sites, there must be a hundred thousand microsites trying to get in on the action—essentially any monkey with a Web site or a blog who's trying to make "millions" by running Google AdSense.

As you've probably guessed, I'm not a fan of the Content Network. I would love to be persuaded otherwise, but for me it has never worked. I find I don't get the click-throughs, and when I do, they don't convert. This could of course just be the industries and specific Web sites I've been promoting through AdWords, but I remain unconvinced. Certainly give it a try, but I strongly recommend turning Content Network off when you launch a new campaign for the simple reason that there are so many variables affecting your AdWords campaign and you need to try to remain in control as much as possible. Being able to measure your CTR is one of those variables. If everything is working well through Google Search, feel free to expand across the Google Network. You'll be able to track very quickly whether the inclusion of your ads on the network is helping or hindering your performance.

If you do feel that Search Network and Content Network are something you'd like to pursue, please go ahead, but I urge you to set up separate campaigns to manage your ads: one for Google Search, one for Content Network, and one for Search Network. You need to keep the CTRs separate so that it is clear what is working for you and where—in terms of understanding your ROI, with a separate campaign you'll be able to make a direct correlation between the cost of advertising and sales as a direct result without having to decipher the figures.

The beauty of the separate campaigns is that it is also easier to manage your bids—which may differ wildly, depending on an ad's destination. I've found the click-throughs from Content Network to be particularly haphazard and those users to be noncommittal, and therefore I'm far less willing to bid at the higher end of the scale. Without doubt, the best "quality" users are those generated through Google Search, so this should always be your major focus unless real sales data prove that your ads and business buck the trend and work best through the Content Network or Search Network.

In defense of the Content Network, its strongest plus point, in my opinion, is, depending on the partner site, the ability to display *image ads* and even *video ads*.

I'll address video ads at the end of Chapter 7 because I think some very exciting things are about to happen with Google AdWords and the embracing of video ads, and certainly the use of image ads, which are going to be of significant benefit to certain industries—not the least those whose business is images, imagery, and related commerce.

Make Sense of AdSense

Those of you who wish to follow the path of advertising via Google's Content Network should bear in mind the types of sites that run Google AdSense. Although there are exceptions to the rule, more often than not these are sites that don't sell products or services themselves, and therefore the revenue they receive from serving AdSense ads and other advertising represents their entire income stream. Generally, they are content providers. It is therefore likely that the ads will be placed in a prominent position (high up on the page)—the trick is to make your ad fit in with the surrounding site. It won't always be the case, but many of the sites running AdSense are forum, portal, or specialist interest sites focused on or concerned with a specific issue—e.g., www.writers.net, a Web site for existing and aspiring writers, runs AdSense. To encourage users to click on my ad from a Content Network page rather than a Google Search result page is going to require a slightly different approach to make my ad fit in.

Research the sites and choose which ones you want to appear on rather than trying to cast your net wide—if you know where you're going to be, you can tailor your ads to speak to that specific audience, which is going to be more likely to click on a specific ad tailored for them than on a generic ad that's just fishing for clicks. Once you have a few weeks of activity clocked up, the reporting tool will show at a glance which sites you're appearing on and the conversion tracker will indicate whether the impressions are converting to click-throughs for you. Remove yourself from the deadwood and improve the ads on your revised list of sites.

Daily Budget

Please note that this is the budget you are prepared to spend per day, not how much you are prepared to spend per click. The bigger your budget is, the longer it will take for you to spend it and therefore the more impressions your ad will receive, which increases the chances of users clicking through. Your budget is spent only when a user clicks on your ad; it does not depend on how many times your ad is shown (this is the number of impressions). Google will determine, by using its own algorithm, how often to show your ad on the basis of (1) your total budget and (2) the price you are prepared to pay per click.

Let's say you have a budget of $10 per day. Just to keep the numbers nice and simple, you are bidding $0.10 per click for the keyword "garden gnome." To continue to keep things simple, this is the only keyword you are bidding on and you have only one ad. Google's algorithm will determine (based on a number of factors that include your own ad's previous performance and the performance of your competitors' ads) that on average your ad is clicked on five times for every hundred times it is shown. Or, in the terminology you're beginning to familiarize yourself with, your ad gets a click-through rate of 5 percent. Therefore, over the course of a day, if your ad is served to 2,000 users, at a CTR of 5 percent, you can expect 100 of them to click through to your site. Now, your own Web site stats should be able to tell you what your conversion ratio is (i.e., the number of visitors to your Web site against the number who complete a purchase). Let's say you have a conversion of 5 percent (i.e., among every 100 visitors to your site, five of them purchase something). Let's also say that the average spend on your site is $25. You can quickly assess that your AdWords campaign cost you $10 for that day and resulted in sales of $125. If this were your business, you'd be pretty happy with that return on investment and probably would look to double your AdWords spend to see if the trend in sales also doubled. Similarly, if you found that your budget of $10 was resulting in only one or even no sales, you'd quickly want to alter your ad and/or your destination Uniform Resource Locator (URL). Otherwise, you'd find yourself quickly broke.

The hardest thing to decide about your daily budget is what figure to put on it. There is no "one size fits all" answer. On the one hand, you don't want to overcommit cash on unproven ads for keywords you have not worked with before. If the ads are getting click-throughs but those click-throughs aren't converting into customers, you're going to be burning through your daily budget quickly with little or no reward. On the other hand, if you don't invest enough, especially in the first weeks and months, your ads may not be served up enough to give you a clear indication of what the interest is or whether your ads are working.

Thankfully, Google will suggest, on the basis of the keywords you have selected, a recommended daily budget. This figure may be tons higher than you are prepared to spend, may be only slightly higher, or may even be lower than the figure you had in mind. The important thing, certainly for the initial two weeks when you are building up your data, is to try to spend as close to the recommended budget as you can. This figure really isn't based on Google trying to monetize your account for all it is worth; it's based on an algorithm of what activity has been like for ads using those keywords in the past. Google will have a good idea of your potential CTR, and the budget will reflect a realistic amount of click-throughs so that both you and Google can benefit from a long and fruitful relationship. It could be that after two weeks you feel the budget needs to be reduced or increased—at least after two weeks you have some real data to help you make that decision, as opposed to just making an educated guess.

Delivery Method

This determines at which time and frequency over a 24-hour period your ad is shown. If you're starting a campaign for the first time, I recommend choosing "Standard," but there may be reason to select "Accelerated."

Standard: show ads evenly over time

This is the default setting. Google will determine, on the basis of your daily budget, how often it needs to show your ad for there to be enough clicks to reach your daily budget. This is not an exact science, and therefore you may not receive enough clicks that day to exhaust your budget. However, your ad will be shown throughout the 24-hour period, giving users the opportunity to see your ad whether they are searching Google during the day or at night.

Accelerated: show ads as quickly as possible

Choose this option if you are determined to spend your budget each day. Google will display your ad more often, with the intention that the budget be utilized fully. Once the daily budget has been exhausted, the ad will be removed until the next day. There is no guarantee that the budget will be spent because, of course, users have to click on the ad for the charge to be made.

Personally, I have always used Standard as it gives an ad a fair chance of catching users throughout any particular day. I have met a number of heavy AdWords advertisers who start new campaigns with Accelerated—their thinking is that they will get essential performance data about their ads more quickly. If they have set to Accelerated and they're not getting through their budget, they know that there's something wrong with the ad message and immediately make changes. Conversely, if their budget is being used up within a couple of hours, they're not getting any more impressions for the rest of the day. This—after checking that the users who have clicked through have become prospects by signing up for something or become customers by buying something—quickly points to the need to increase the daily budget to get more users. Similarly, if the users are all coming through fast and furious but not becoming prospects or customers, both the ad and the destination URL need to be looked at and optimized.

Target Audiences

Languages

This is simply a way to tell Google in which language or languages your ads are written and therefore who to serve them to. It really is a waste of time to have a campaign entirely in English and then select Russian even if you are selling Russian products or products that are of interest to Russian speakers. Use Locations to determine which country the ad is served to; Languages is for languages.

Locations

This is the country in which your potential customer lives. Now, I'm guessing that most of you reading this book will want to choose the United States as a geographic location to begin with, so in this case your ad will be shown to users who search www.google.com. If you added Spain as a location, the ad also would be served to users searching on www.google.es, and so on. Obviously, as marketers and optimists, we think people in every country around the world deserve to buy our products or benefit from our services, but you'll be wasting time and money serving your ads to the wrong sort of user. Although impressions don't cost you anything per se, they do have an effect on the performance of your ad in terms of your click-through rate and therefore your ad's viability and longevity.

When running a company called Toytopia, I was convinced there were thousands of British expats living in Spain who would love to buy gifts for their loved ones back in the United Kingdom through a UK-based Web site, and so I started an AdWords campaign that focused on the location of Spain with the ads written in English. It didn't work. Instead I focused my efforts solely on the United Kingdom and Ireland, and later, once the site was translated into Spanish, I added Spain as a location again (along with a .es microsite tailored to the expats), and this time it did work.

Don't try to scattershoot your marketing—keep it limited to your core audience or audiences and expand once you've proved that your campaign works in one location or a handful of locations.

Keyword Bidding

The most important factor in this relationship for both you and Google is the money. Google wants to maximize its revenue, and you want to keep your campaign costs to a minimum. Google, in my opinion, plays it pretty fair—the cost of your campaign basically comes down to supply and demand for the keywords you are interested in bidding on. If it's really niche and only a few other advertisers are bidding on that keyword, you're going to enjoy a low cost per click. If, however, there are already a lot of other advertisers all wanting to attract clicks for the same keyword, your Google AdWords campaign is going to be a whole lot more expensive. Google gives you the tools to experiment with your pricing, and with the daily or monthly cap on spending, your campaign can't get out of control. If your ad works, Google will reward you with a lower average cost per click, but only you will know if it's working. You might be a specialist software reseller and your keyword might be costing $10 per click, but if you are making $2,000 per sale, it's a reasonable cost per sale—but that's not the case if you're making only $20 per sale.

Manual (or Maximum) Bidding

This is the most common choice, as it gives you the most control over your bidding, especially if you have numerous campaigns and groups that you may want to work in different ways (e.g., an ad group that you are deliberately bidding low on to test the waters or because you find you get a better CTR when displayed at position 3 or 4 rather than position 1). It is important to note that the amount you enter as your bid is the *most* you are willing to pay per click and not necessarily what you will pay—that will depend on what other advertisers are paying and the performance of your ads. Bid only what you can afford!

Cost per Acquisition Bid

This is a handy little feature that was introduced recently to complement Google's Conversion Optimizer tool. If you grant access to Google to monitor your users' behavior from click-through to (one hopes) purchase or sign-up, this style of bidding may appeal. The idea is that you bid on how much you are willing to pay for a conversion as opposed to a click-through. For all businesses, converting a user into a customer is the true indicator of whether an AdWord campaign is working—click-throughs are worthless unless they end up as sales.

Generally, the cost per acquisition bidding will start a lot higher than the cost per click, but this is an all-encompassing fee that allows for impressions with no clicks and clicks with no purchase, and it boils down to what you are willing to pay for a new customer. Again, the amount you bid is the *maximum* you are willing to pay for the acquisition.

Please note that to use this bidding option you must have already signed up to Conversion Optimizer and (at the time of this writing) had at least 200 conversions within the last 30 days.

Budget Optimizer (AdWords-Lite)

This is certainly the option to choose if you're already feeling overwhelmed by the array of choices and decisions you need to make in terms of setting up and running an AdWords campaign. With Budget Optimizer you decide on a monthly budget, sit back, and relax. . . . Google will optimize the display of all your ads to try to get your budget spent on clicks. It works fine if your only goal is to maximize number of clicks you receive in any specific month, but it leaves you with very little control. In fairness, you will spend your budget and will get traffic. At first glance, that may seem quite attractive, but you will lose the ability to specify the times your ads are shown, which may affect your conversion rate and your preferences about the position in which your ad is displayed, which in turn will affect your cost per click.

Preferred Cost Bidding

If you are looking for a bit more control over your ad spend while still maintaining control over your ad's timing, Preferred Cost Bidding allows you to dictate more closely how much your average cost per click will be, as opposed to setting a maximum bid and then waiting for Google to tell you what your average cost per click turned out to be.

Preferred Cost Bidding works best once you actually have an AdWords history—i.e., if over the past few months your ads have performed better when you've been paying an average price of, say, $0.65, you might want to stipulate this as your preferred bid. If, however, you are new to AdWords, the flexibility of stipulating a maximum bid will return far more useful data in terms of the best position and best time of day and more flexibility to compete with competitors who may be altering their bid prices daily or weekly.

Keeping the Focus Narrow

I can't stress enough how good management of your AdWords campaign or campaigns will pay off in the end. This starts with the way you structure and name your ads and filters down to the amount and detail of the keywords you are bidding on. One advertisement simply will not be sufficient to cover the aims, goals, and desires of every user searching for all those keywords—their interest is too broad, and the ad will fail because it's too vague to entice users to click through or because too many users click through but don't do anything on your site, costing you a tremendous amount of cash for no return.

It is far better to have a single ad completely tailored for each keyword and thus have a portfolio of 50 ads running to cover your keyword range than to pin your hopes and the success of your AdWords campaign on the back of a couple of generic "they'll do" crowd-pleasers.

It does take time to set up numerous ads and it does take time to monitor their performance and continue to test and tweak them to improve that performance, but it's time well spent and can make the difference between e-business success and abject failure.

Position Preference

On first appearance, this might seem to be a somewhat strange option. In everything we do, especially when it has anything whatsoever to do with the words "Google," "ranking," and "position," we all crave the top spot. To be number 1 seems to be the king, the alpha, a reason to live! And yet Google offers advertisers the opportunity to shun this coveted position—to actually express a preference for something lower. "Why?" I hear you ask. Well, there is a school of thought that maintains that the top spot or even the top three spots aren't the be-all and end-all. Months of stats regarding previous and existing ad campaigns can show that some ads, for some keywords, in some industries, actually do markedly better in terms of CTR, price to the advertiser, and users' actions once they've clicked through in, say, position 4, 5, or 6 or even position 10. It's strange but true. It could be that Google users are more switched on than many advertisers give them credit for—they know what AdWords are and even how they work and therefore deliberately do not choose to go with the advertiser that is perceived to be bidding the most money per click. Just out of spite, users actually seek out an ad lower down the list and click there instead. There is also a case for saying that some users deliberately ignore the ads placed by Google above the natural search results—perceiving these ads to be sponsored, they are unwilling to click.

Another possibility is that users do not see those ads at all because they blend into the search results, meaning that the users are in fact more likely to click on the ads served on the right-hand side of the page—and if the users click on the top AdWords on the right, that is in fact ad number 3 or 4. For this reason and because Google will show only two or three ads at the top of the search results, by deliberately opting for a preference for position 3 or 4, you may get a better CTR than that of the ads served in position 1 or 2.

The jury's out on this and what works for one business may or may not work for you, but what is clear is that it works enough for Google to offer you the chance to choose a position preference if you want to. Review your ads and experiment with positioning to see what works for you—all the information is there for you to make an informed decision both before and after any change to your ad, and you'll quickly know whether it's working for you.

Don't Get Carried Away

Someone, somewhere will always have a bigger pot of cash than you. That's life; get over it. You might find that the particular keywords you are interested in are already hotly contested and bid prices are high. Don't despair—the number 1 AdWords position is not the only position that means success.

Although it's difficult to concede defeat, you may be able to afford to be only at position 5 or 6. Even so, it's worth entering the race. If you get your ad right and impress Google with a commanding CTR, you will rise up in the rankings without having to spend any more money—and possibly by spending less money.

When you're deciding how much you are willing to bid on a keyword, you would be wise to see what the recommended bid value is. However, this is your campaign, so it is fundamentally your choice. Base your decision on what you can afford and pay attention to the CTR and how those users convert into customers on your site—it could be that you actually make more money for your business with an ad placed at position 6, 7, or 8 than you do when you've broken the bank to be number 1.

Case Study—Logo Warehouse

It's more serendipity than anything else, but it so happens that at the time of writing this book I am also about to launch an online business selling predesigned logo templates and offering a bespoke logo design service—all at very reasonable prices. The Web site is www.logo-warehouse.co.uk, and it will be a useful exercise for you—and for me—to look at examples of what works and what doesn't through the lens of a live and current AdWords campaign.

So, a few weeks before launch, I'm ready to take another look at the current market and begin to make plans about how I'm going to tackle my AdWords campaign. Of course, I looked into the market when I was planning the business, but that was a number of months ago, and as we all know, the entire online landscape can change (both positively and negatively) in a short time span. Hence, this exercise is always worth repeating.

The first thing I need to do is get a feel for the market. There are going to be a number of keywords I'm going to want to bid on (more on this in Chapter 3), but for now let's take a look at "logo templates" and "bespoke logo design," which are the phrases I used to describe the business and which seem as a good a place as any to begin.

Looking at the results shown in Figures 2.1 and 2.2, it's quite clear that I'm not the only player in the market and am certainly not the only one who is interested in AdWords. Fear not; competition is healthy, and seeing so many other companies trying to capture the same market gives me confidence that AdWords works for my industry—if it didn't, do you really think so many companies would continue to pay for a service with little or no return? Yes, it's going to cost me a bit more per click, but I've factored that into my pricing model. Let's get started.

Defining Campaigns and Ad Groups

The ultimate success of your new relationship with Google depends on the perform-ance of your ad campaign; therefore, as you're going to be checking data relating to your campaign a lot over the coming weeks and months, it makes sense to structure your campaign in a logical way. This structure should not be just some way that makes sense to you; it must be in a form that can be explained with ease to a colleague.

Your first major decision therefore is to define a structure that is going to work for you now and that is also scalable. What's best: to create a new *campaign* or a new *ad group*?

Well, the important thing to remember here is the different settings relating to these two choices. Campaigns have "macro"-level settings—your target language or languages, geographic locations, distribution preferences, and start and end dates, plus, of course, a daily budget. You can create up to 25 campaigns. Ad groups have

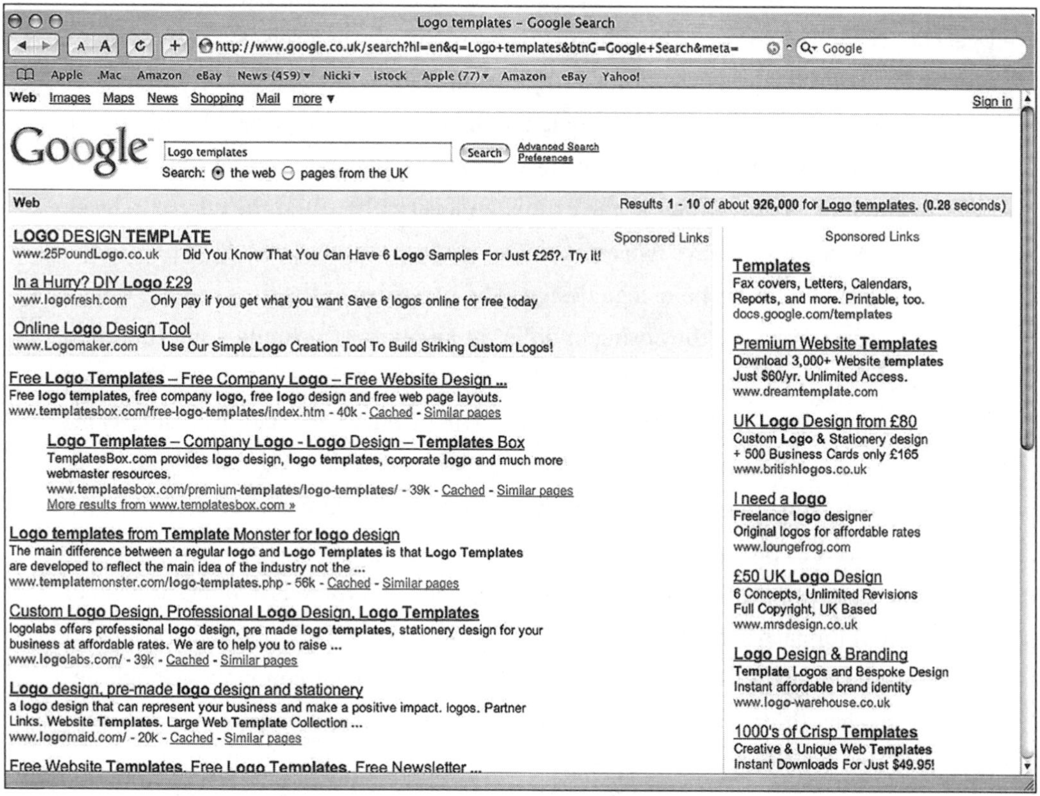

Figure 2.1 The keyword "logo templates" is popular with advertisers—ads are being displayed on the right-hand side of the page but not at the top. I'm guessing that although competition is hot for this keyword, it's not fierce.

"micro"-level settings—your list of keywords, destination URLs, and maximum cost per click (CPC); of course, within the ad group are the ads themselves. There is a maximum level of 100 ad groups within a single campaign.

So what dictates whether a campaign or an ad group is required? It's up to you. What I would say is that to get big, you need to think big and therefore plan for the future and look at everything at the campaign level rather than the ad group level. For Logo Warehouse, I have two campaigns: one for the template logo aspect of the business and one for bespoke logo design. The two sides of the business are different cost centers for me—they bring in different amounts of revenue—and therefore they have separate and very different daily budgets. With my Toytopia business, each "product type" had its own campaign. For instance, we had a distinct campaign for clothing, and within that campaign were several ad groups, such as T-shirts, shoes, and bibs. Similarly, with the toys, "push-along toys" had its own campaign, as did "plush toys."

Separate campaigns certainly should be employed if there is a different head of department for each section of your business, and there is no doubt that you should use multiple campaigns if multiple users have access to your company's Google account—the last thing you want is for your campaign performance to suffer because of a colleague's failings!

Setting up more campaigns than you need is not a tremendous problem—after all, it's just an extra click of the mouse to drop down to the ad group level—but not setting up enough campaigns can prove awkward in the future. Managing your

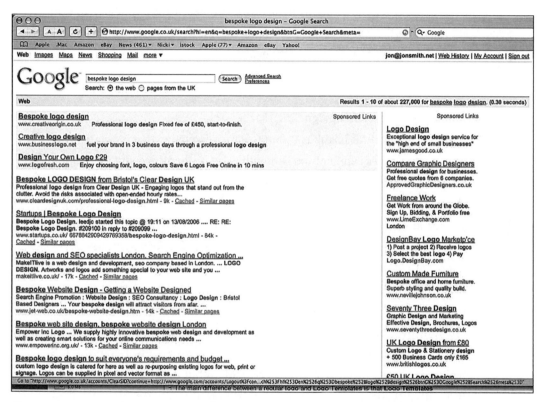

Figure 2.2 The keyword "bespoke logo design" is really popular with advertisers—ads are being displayed on the right-hand side of the page and at the top. I'm guessing that competition for this keyword is fierce.

campaigns and ad groups is straightforward if you make it manageable from the start. You probably will need to make alterations as time progresses, and so it is important to think through how things might evolve.

Logo Warehouse: The Basic Campaign

To get me started as quickly as possible, I want to have a campaign that is easy to measure in terms of effectiveness and not too demanding on my bank account. A common mistake is to try to serve your ad around the world, but if you sell garden gnomes and your Web site is priced in pounds sterling or dollars, it's unlikely that you're going to have many customers in Asia or South America. Also, if your Web site is written in English, there's little point paying for an ad that will display to Japanese users. . . .

There are, of course, exceptions to the rule, and you'll know who and where your market is. But for now, start small and grow into territories rather than trying to use a scattershot approach and hoping that something will stick. If you can't do a good job in your own backyard, you're going to be hard pressed to break into the rest of world. Once you've proved that your AdWords campaign works in the U.S. market, feel free to spread your wings farther afield . . . but not until then!

I'll start with just three ads, all with slightly different messages. Since my business is in the United Kingdom, my target countries are the United Kingdom and Ireland, and so as not to alienate readers, I will be using a modest budget of $5 per day (or about $150 per month) to get my AdWords campaign under way. I'm still a few weeks away from launch, but I want my ads to be ready to go. The moment my site goes live, I'll give Google my payment details, and the ads will be served (see Figures 2.3 through 2.6).

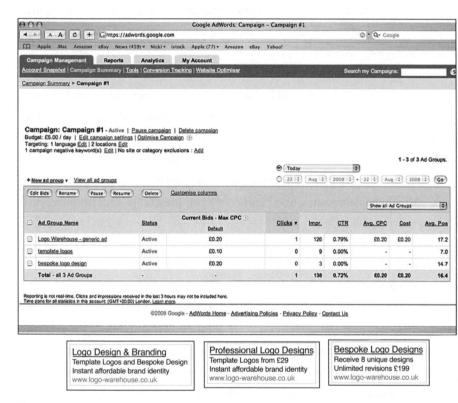

Figure 2.3 My basic campaign has just three advertisements (Figures 2.4, 2.5, and 2.6). They will be displayed only in the United Kingdom and Ireland, and my entire budget is capped at $5 per day.

Figures 2.4-2.6 Advertisement 1: This is my generic ad, focusing on both template logos and bespoke design. Advertisement 2: This is my "template" ad, which mentions only template designs. Advertisement 3: This is my "bespoke" ad, which focuses on the bespoke aspect of the business.

The differences between the ads are very slight, but it's these subtleties of language and change of focus that can make or break an AdWords campaign. In my research into the logo design market, it became evident that price was a major factor. So, to compete effectively, it's clear that I must be up-front about my pricing, which I have done in my example ads.

With any new campaign and first venture into Google AdWords, I want to stress that you should start small and build up your campaign rather than trying to be all things to all people and spending a small fortune on an ineffective—or, worse, inconclusive—campaign. Data from your early weeks will quickly confirm what keywords are working for you and, more important, what *negative* keywords you need to employ to improve your CTR. Start off too big, with an unmanageable list of keywords, and you'll become swamped and confused; inevitably, the campaign will be both expensive and a failure.

Reinventing the Wheel?

Testing and rewriting are critical to a successful AdWords campaign—not just your own ads but the ads and the activity of your competitors. This book (in fact any book) cannot tell you how to write the perfect ad for your business, but in a strange way, your competitors can. Start with the basics—type in one of the keywords you are bidding on already or intend to bid on and pay attention to the results. This test can be repeated as often as you like: I would try for every two hours to allow for any competitor settings to show themselves, such as accelerated delivery or a limited daily spend coming into effect. What you will notice is either the same ad (or a range of ads from the same business) coming up on top or an eclectic mix of ads all changing position with each search. Over a number of days and especially over the coming weeks, a pattern will emerge. If there is a consistent ad or a selection of consistent ads always in the top spots, it's pretty safe to assume that those ads are working for the advertiser. Learn from them, emulate them, and ultimately improve on them.

This is not cheating. It's not taking the easy option—it's competitor analysis. What phrases are they using? What aspects of their ads can you incorporate into yours? What your competitors are doing should form the basis of your own campaign. This becomes your opening gambit, and then the real testing begins as you start to incorporate small alterations that, one hopes, will become improvements, resulting in a higher CTR and, again one hopes, a lower bid price.

Be sure to empty your cache and/or temporary Internet files before any test. Otherwise, you run the risk of seeing a cached version of the Google Search results page.

Ad Position

Every industry is different and every keyword is different, but chances are that there are at least a few competitors running AdWords campaigns for the same keywords you are using. A bit of competition is healthy and should even be encouraged. However, it gets messy when there are more than ten advertisers, because there are only ten positions for AdWords ads on any search results page. Therefore, if your ad is positioned at number 11 or beyond, it's not being displayed on the first page of those results, and I'm afraid that's not of much value to you. It's certainly true that some users will click through to page 2 and beyond to find what they are looking for, but their focus at this stage will very much be on the organic or natural listings, and they probably will be searching for something very specific—so your ad's not going to work effectively.

Now, it could be that you're happy with the cheap bid price and the very occasional click-through—but don't forget, if the CTR drops too low or never picks up, Google is going to disable the ad, so it's little use being in that position. Personally, if I can't afford to be in the top ten ad positions, I kill the ad and look at investing the cash in niche keywords in which I can compete.

Number 1 Isn't Everything

Remember that as hard as it might be to believe, the number 1 spot isn't always the best. Later on in the book we'll see how being number 3 or number 4 actually can produce a far higher ROI for your business, but for now I just want to warn against getting sucked into a bidding war with another advertiser because you both want to be number 1. It happens easily—either you come along and decide to oust the current incumbent by bidding higher and he or she responds or you are enjoying the top spot and a young pretender comes along and outbids you; before long, you both increase your bids, which results in counterbid after counterbid. Now that war's broken out, the two advertisers fighting for the top spot are paying an average price per click of $3 or $4 or more, yet the bidding for position 3 remains at a modest $0.45. The advertiser is still getting click-throughs at position 3, and we can guess that those click-throughs are converting to customers on the site. So while you two monkeys are having a private spat over the number 1 spot, the price per new customer is far higher than you should be paying.

Only Google wins when there's a bidding war. Set yourself a limit—a percentage amount you are willing to go up to from your initial bid—and stick to it. Once there's somebody out there who's willing to keep on upping the ante, back away. Positions 3, 4, and 7 are just as viable and can be just as profitable.

A Word of Warning

Click fraud happens. Now, the good news is that Google has tools in place to detect an obvious attempt by a single IP address (read: a nefarious individual, probably a competitor) to click on your ad multiple times, which ordinarily would cost you a lot of money. When click fraud is detected, you will get a refund, but it's still in your interest to monitor your log files for IP addresses on click-throughs and to notice any suspicious activity. Low-level fraud will get through undetected and will cost you money, but I'm afraid there's not a tremendous amount you can do about it. No doubt when you were researching your keywords, you clicked on some ads to see what lay at the destination URL, and competitors will do the same thing to you. During the process of writing this book I have clicked on thousands of ads with absolutely no intention of buying anything from the advertisers.

It's frustrating, it's expensive (very, if you happen to be in an industry in which clicks for your keywords cost many dollars each), and it will affect your CTR negatively. But please, don't be tempted to exacerbate the problem by becoming trigger-happy yourself. It's not big, it's not clever, and it doesn't impress the girls. And let's face it—it wouldn't take much for Google to match the IP address of your AdWords account with a problem IP address for one of your competitors. At best, your campaign will be shut down instantaneously and your Web site removed from the Google index; at worst, you could be on the receiving end of a lawsuit.

document, efficiency, electronic, female, hap
ook, people, person, plan, planning, pretty, se
, woman, work, young communication, comp
, web, corporate, debate, dialogue, document,
mpany, job, business, people, plan, prof
pretty, sensual, service, corporate, people, w
woman, work, young, communication, comp
e, dialogue, document, efficiency, electronic.
ptop, matching, notebook, people, person, pl
mart, smile, sophisticated, straight, web, won

3

The Importance of Keywords

In Praise of the Long Tail

I love the long tail. Focusing on the long tail of products has allowed companies such as Borders, Barnes and Noble, and Toys R Us to enter the busy and competitive book-DVD-games retail market and become serious players in only a few years despite the perceived belief that Amazon has online sales all sewn up.

In terms of AdWords and choosing your keywords, the long tail is of paramount importance, especially if you are looking to find a niche for yourself or if budget constraints mean that you can't compete with the big boys in terms of the critical (read: generic) keywords in your particular industry.

Google offers a keyword search as part of the "AdWords Dashboard," but it's worth bidding on words you've thought of yourself—it's your industry, after all, and that knowledge you have of the market is just as important as Google's view of the related words. It's also worth looking elsewhere for keyword suggestions, such as www.nichebot.com and www.wordtracker.com. Both of these sites recently started charging for their services, but if you're taking your AdWords campaign seriously, it's a necessary expense.

There are top-level keywords in every industry. As an online toy seller I was obsessed with the keyword "toys," but it quickly became apparent that I was up against Toys 'R' Us and ToyMaster even though we were in different markets. On long-term marketing spend, I simply couldn't compete. The click-throughs we did get when we paid more than the usual price for the keyword "toys" weren't converting to sales. What was the matter? The answer was that we had a specialist offering—traditional-style wooden toys, finger puppets, pram toys, and off-the-wall clothing and footwear. The simple fact was, people who typed in the word "toys" were looking for the latest craze, invariably made out of plastic, which had been advertising on the television. That wasn't the sort of stuff we sold. Okay, we sold toys, but not the toys those people were looking for.

The answer: Go niche. Be specific. Explore the long tail. I optimized our ads to be specific, not generic—"wooden toys," "push-along toys," and so on—and the results were staggering. Suddenly we were enjoying a higher CTR and, more important, a higher conversion ratio. In simple terms, we were attracting the right sorts of customers, those who *were* interested in buying from our offering, and more of them were committing to purchase.

Once you have decided on your long-tail keywords, don't forget to divide them into sensible and focused ad groups. Only then can you track how effective they are.

Ad Group Convention

We all get a bit carried away when first setting up an AdWords campaign—we want our ad to be visible in every country and want it to be displayed whenever a huge list of keywords is queried by a user. Stop! Think!

AdWords works best when a targeted ad is precision tailored for one keyword or a small selection of keywords. One generic ad serving 50 keywords won't be all things to all people; it will just be ignored (and quite quickly disabled by Google). Or, worse, it will attract a high CTR but with users then realizing they don't want anything to do with you or your Web site—after they have cost you money.

It's far better to break down your selection of keywords into small, themed, easy-to-manage groups. It doesn't matter how many groups you create—you can have up to 100 ads per ad group—just make the task manageable and logical, and this will result in your ads for those groups being far more effective.

Internet Users Are Cash-Rich and Time-Poor and Can't Spell

We are all guilty of using Google Search without a care in the world for spelling, grammar, or punctuation. How many times have you typed something like "cassic cars" and Google has helpfully asked, "Did you mean classic cars?" We all do it, and that's something you should remember when you're looking to expand your keywords and the size of your campaign.

Negative Keywords

I know it's natural to want to cast your net as widely as possible and to strive to welcome all newcomers warmly. And yes, it's correct that we don't truly know what a user's actions are going to be until that user hits your site. But I can tell you that after a few weeks, when you start seeing the money going out for click-throughs that aren't converting, you tend to lose whatever egalitarian views you might have had and get all fascist.

Negative keywords give you some freedom to limit the kinds of searches, and therefore the kinds of user, you might attract.

Negative keywords allow you to specify when you don't want your ad to be shown. In the example of Logo Warehouse, I charge for the logos on offer, so I want bargain hunters to refrain from clicking on my ads. I've therefore listed "free" as a negative keyword because I'm a business, not a charity.

In the case of my toy business, as well as having a long list of keywords I did want to bid on—"push-along toys," "wooden building blocks," "puppets," and so on—it was very easy to keep the wrong sorts of customers away by determining what they might accidentally think I might sell—"Transformers," "Pokemon," "Sex-Toys," and so forth. The negative keyword list was very long indeed.

If the glut of phone calls we received from customers asking for the latter products was any indication of demand, we must have saved thousands and thousands of dollars in what would have been wasted click-throughs on our AdWords. And if you're wondering why we didn't decide to sell these products if demand was so

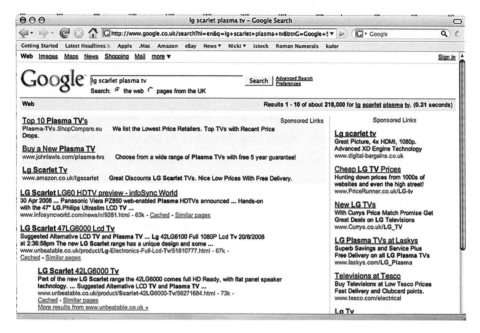

Figure 3.1 The ad I will click on will be the ad that best represents my search—in this case, the ads that acknowledge not just LG (the manufacturer) but the specific Scarlet range.

high, the truth is that we considered it, but the market is very faddish and the markup on those products is rubbish.

Your negative keyword list will grow constantly because you won't think of everything at first. It is only as the clicks begin to come through and you are able to analyze the actual phrases being used that you'll notice a pattern of searchers who enter certain words, along with the keyword you're targeting, but are not converting once they've clicked through. These searches are costing you money, and you need to add the problem keywords to your negative list. If you sell products or services at a regular or premium rate, deter the bargain hunters from the outset by including negative keywords such as "discount," "free," "cheap," and "bargain." If you sell only ceramic garden gnomes, add "plastic" and "wooden" as negative keywords.

The more specific you can be with your description in your ad, the more likely it is that you'll get the right sort of user clicking through and, ideally, becoming a customer. If you're selling plasma TVs, run specific ads for each of the brand names you carry—and on top of that, include the model or series type. For example, I recently saw an advertisement on TV for the Scarlet Plasma TV from LG. I wanted more information, and I turned to Google. Figure 3.1 shows what I found.

So I had a few choices. There were a couple of links in the organic listings that mentioned both LG (the manufacturer) and the Scarlet range of TVs, and there were two ads which did the same thing. My natural instinct on this occasion was to click the ad placed at the top of the right-hand side—the ad in position 4. Not only has the use of dynamic keywords for the headline confirmed that this ad will answer my need, the brand and the range are reinforced within the ad content.

succentor /sək'

succinere acco

success /sək's

nation of atte

position, or

achievement.

successus]

4

Getting Started with AdWords

What Determines Whether Your Ad Appears
at the Top of the Page or on the Right?

Nothing . . . well, nothing you can alter or influence. It's Google's thing: Sometimes all the ads are placed on the right side of the page, and sometimes there are two at the top of the page. These are not separate or more expensive positions; they're AdWords ads. It's just that they tend to be displayed when a particular keyword is popular and therefore there's a lot of advertiser demand. Look at it as a reward scheme—the keywords that are real moneymakers for Google are worth encouraging. The companies that are prepared to bid the most are making the most money per click for Google, and thus it makes complete sense for Google to give them the top spot—quite literally at the top of the page. If the keywords you're bidding on are in low demand or relatively cheap, your ad will be displayed on the right of the page.

Toeing the ##!!!!L@@K & FEEL!!!!### Line

Going back to Chapter 1 briefly, you'll remember that part of Google's success and the reason users came back again and again was its refreshingly simple and clean look. Compared with the noisy Yahoo! and AltaVista home pages, Google's clean white space made search almost a pleasure, and users flocked to use its service, making Google the number 1 search engine very quickly. Google's home page is possibly the most valuable real estate on the World Wide Web. I have no doubt that lots and lots of companies have offered eye-watering amounts of cash to be advertised there and have all been refused. Google doesn't like noise. Google doesn't like garishness. Google doesn't like blatant commercialism. Google's business model and huge success have proved categorically that simplicity works effectively, and that's why Google ain't going to tolerate any shenanigans from you!

Familiarize yourself with Google's AdWords Program Service Agreement—it is strictly enforced. In a nutshell, the look and feel of your ads should err on the side of caution. Any ads that make excessive use of CAPS and exclamation points (!!!!!!!) will be removed—in fact, the rule is that you're allowed to use only one exclamation mark! Don't be tempted to try it to see how long your ad will last (I've done that for you, and about three weeks is the best I've managed). It's a waste of your time when you could be using and benefiting from a "proper" ad that's bringing prospects to your site. Google does have the power and the right to cancel your AdWords account completely, especially if you are a habitual offender—and let's face it, they have the technology to check your organic listings and tactics easily too. It doesn't take a genius to realize that if you're pushing it in terms of your AdWords campaign, that may lead to a closer investigation of your overall relationship with Google. The net result could be a total removal from the Google index, and you really don't want that! Play it safe, play it cool, and craft your ads well.

Keep the Message Going

There must be a relevant relationship between the sales message you display in your ad and the content of the page the user finds at the destination URL. It's not good enough to mention sexy bras in your ad and then point users to your generic lingerie home page. Point the user to a specific page on your site that reinforces the ad. In this case, bring the user to your bra page or to a specific bra product detail page that shows bras selling for the price you quoted in the ad.

Don't expect users to arrive at your home page and willingly navigate through your site to find the offer, the deal, or the free gift you promised in your ad. If what they want isn't there to greet them on their arrival at the destination URL, they are going to abandon your site, and although you'll get the credit in your CTR, you won't have made any money—only lost it.

The Importance of Quality

Google's aim is to serve the best search results to its users. Along with those search results come AdWords, and Google is obsessed with ensuring that the ads are relevant and beneficial to the users to avoid damaging the hard work that's been done in building Google Search. That's why your ads are scored on relevancy and receive a quality score, that's why there are strict editorial rules, and that's why frequent offenders have their accounts suspended!

The good news is that if you are playing by the rules and your ads are targeted and effective, you will be rewarded. This is one way your actions can speak louder than your competitor's fat wallet.

Personally, I always start my bidding high, based on what, if anything, competitors are doing around my keywords of choice. This makes the early click-throughs expensive, but it serves a number of purposes. First, it lets users and competitors know that my business or my client's business has arrived. Second, this might cause a panic, and over the next few days there will be a bidding war or frenzy with competitors altering their bidding tactics and even the content of their ads. (At this point, I don't react; I just let it happen and see where I stand once the dust has settled.) Third, because I've gone in high, it's likely that my generosity to Google's war chest will be rewarded by a high rank (position 1 or 2) and users are clicking through. Now, assuming that I've gotten my sales message right and the content on the destination URL is to the users' liking, I am building my reputation with Google in the form of a high CTR percentage and a good quality score and, most important, converting users into consumers, so the extra business is paying for the inflated ad prices.

Give it a week and then drop your bid price—you might be surprised. As often as not, you can come in with, say, a 10 percent lower bid per click and still maintain your position! Quality score, relevancy, and testing really pay off. If you've held your position for a week and still are getting a favorable CTR, try it again: Drop your bid by another 10 percent. It can go on like this and you will continue to save money while maintaining your position and the ad's effectiveness—or you can suddenly drop to position 50. As soon as that happens, increase your bid price again and you'll be back up the list. But think of all the money you've saved over the weeks (across all of your ad groups) by shaving off 10 percent here and there.

It might work for your keywords; it might not. Try it and find out.

5

Ad Groups
and Advanced AdWords

Google Editor—More Control

It's free and it works. If you want to be truly in control of your AdWords campaign, the first thing you are going to need, if you haven't downloaded it already, is AdWords Editor—Google's campaign management application. You can read about it at www.google.com/intl/en/adwordseditor/.

The main advantage of using AdWords Editor over making the alterations manually through your Google AdWords account is the ability to make mass changes and alterations over a selection of ad groups and individual ads. It also makes managing large AdWords accounts more straightforward, especially if you are working with a long list of keywords.

Your Schedule

It's all in the planning. Good campaign management requires constant tinkering, rewriting, monitoring of data, and reacting and interacting with Google, your competitors, and your ads. But it's not going to work if you don't have a plan!

It's best to think of your AdWords campaign in terms of cycles. These can be cycles that your business already employs, such as weekly, monthly, quarterly, and seasonally, but decide now how you are going to operate and stick to it.

With any campaign I am running, I create a number of review dates. These are cycles, determined by a mix of calendar constraints and experience with AdWords. They may or may not work for you, but this might be a good place to start as you become more familiar with AdWords.

Before any testing and during testing, be sure to empty your cache.

• **Weekly**

Positioning analysis

On each of your keywords, what is your average position?

Position doctoring

Any ad that is lower than it was the week before needs improving: Alter the ad text or alter your bid. With any ads that have remained static or have improved their average position, it is up to you whether you want to alter them. (Personally, I employ split, or A/B, testing in these circumstances and see if I can improve again on an ad's performance. More on this in Chapter 7.)

- **Monthly**

  Rerun a keyword search

  Find out what users are looking for and make sure your AdWords ads are tailored to those keywords.

  Add to negative keywords

  With a month of data, you'll be able to see if there are some keywords still slipping through with no conversion—add those problem keywords to your negative list.

- **Quarterly**

With three months of data, you can really see what's working and what's not. Even if your ads or ad groups are performing well enough not to have been disabled, they may not be working well for you and giving you a strong ROI. Make a decision: You can continue with alterations and testing or kill the group and reassign the budget to another group or campaign.

Document Everything!

It may seem like a waste of time and a lot of the information is of course visible within your AdWords account, but I'm a big fan of cut and paste—all the information I need is transferred into an Excel spreadsheet and tailored the way I like it. The date of the next review is fixed, and I stick to it.

You can go easy on yourself and start each new cycle on Monday or the first of the month or follow the seasons for your quarterly tasks—personally, I like to mix it up a bit. Most people make their alterations on a Friday or, more likely, a Monday. (I prefer to make weekly changes on a Wednesday so that I can react both to my own ads' performance and to any alterations my competitors have made.) The same goes for monthly checks—I pick a random day of the month (usually the nineteenth) and avoid the first or last week of any month, when most of my competitors are making their own alterations.

Your Ads' Schedule

There's a host of reasons why interest in your ad is determined by the day of the week—you may be aware of them or you may not. What's important is to look out for this information. Similarly, you may wish to show your ads only over the weekend or only during the week. It may defy logic, but if over a number of weeks your conversion ratio drops significantly on Tuesday and Thursday, it's fine to turn off your ads on those days. Your CTR will be calculated only on the days when the ad is showing; thus, if you've got a good CTR, your bid price is going to go down. Hence, you may be getting more customers more cheaply by advertising only two days a week as opposed to a full week. The beauty of having separate ad groups or even campaigns is that you can have different ads running for different days of the week if you wish.

Playing with the Big Boys

There are times when, try as you might, you've exhausted every keyword, no matter how specialized or niche, and it's still an expensive market to be entering. Does this mean you should pack your bags and think of starting again in a completely different industry? Absolutely not! It may mean you need to rethink your pricing model to incorporate the higher cost per new customer or that you need to revise your forecasts on the basis of customer acquisition via Google AdWords, but as the lottery people say, you've got to be in it to win it. So keep going. The key is to spend even more time and effort testing and tracking your campaigns—every penny really will count, and those pennies need to be working for you in terms of conversions. Fear not: All the tools and information you need are there for you to use—next, we'll see how.

When Things Are Working, Bid Higher!

At first, this might seem a bit odd because your main focus is creating ads that work well and then trying to find ways to shave a bit off the cost while still keeping a good CTR and a good conversion rate. However, there's a lot to be said for increasing your bid on ads that have been working well for you. At a basic level, this might throw the competition and price them out of the market. Also, if Google notices that this ad is performing well, it's going to favor it over others.

It could be that you increase your bid on an ad that was performing well at position 6 and suddenly it finds itself bumped up to position 1 or 2. That might happen because you raised your bid by as little as 5 cents! If you had competed through the regular bid channel, you might have had to pay many times that to achieve a higher spot.

Deter Unwanted Click-Throughs

This also may seem odd, but as much as you want users to click through to your site, you don't want them if they're not the right sorts of users. By including a deterrent within your ad—such as a higher price or another barrier to entry—you are encouraging those who can afford your product or service and deterring those who can't.

Click-throughs are of value to you only if those users then do something on your site—register, contact you, or purchase. Everyone else is no more than a casual visitor, and too many of them will cost you money with no ROI.

For example, Espressio's flagship product is our extra-large hardback "Photo book. Reasonably priced at $25.57" (see Figure 5.1 for the British version of the ad).

For some users, that's too high—and therefore we don't want their clicks—so quoting the price in the ad both attracts the users we do want and deters the users we don't.

Coffee Table Photo Book
Impressive 30cm x 30cm
Delivered to your door £17.99
www.espressio.co.uk/xlarge

Figure 5.1

Improving the Click-Through Rate

Using delimiters has improved my CTR on campaigns considerably over the years. The technique is completely *white hat SEO* and simply involves using a simple pair of punctuation marks as *delimiters*—quotes (". . .") and brackets ([. . .])—to narrow your focus and make sure your advertisement is served to the niche you want. (We'll look at using negative keywords later.)

Let's say you're bidding on "wooden toys"—an old favorite of mine from the days when I ran Toytopia, which specialized in wooden toys, among other things.

You should bid on it in not one way but three:

1. wooden toys
2. "wooden toys"
3. [wooden toys]

Now you are bidding on wooden toys as a broad term, which means that your ad will appear any time those two words are typed in as part of a search, in any order. You also are bidding on "wooden toys," which includes any search entry that includes those two words, but only in that order. Finally, you are bidding on [wooden toys], which includes searches placed on only those two words in that exact order.

Once you've added these delimiters to your search terms, you'll get a much clearer idea of what kinds of specific searches people are doing on the terms you're bidding on.

This technique is effective because when you bid on a "broad" search term, you are competing against ads that are targeting all sorts of unrelated terms. You see, the search item wooden toys is competing with all ads targeting the keywords "toys" and "wooden." Broad searches can be dangerous in that they can become very expensive and can mean that you are forced to compete against competitors on the more costly terms for all manner of queries unless you have a huge list of negative keywords. Using bounded or delimited searches narrows the field and reduces the overall and/or average competition for ad space, so your cost to maintain the same average position should drop in comparison to the cost of an unbounded term.

Using Dynamic Keywords

Dynamic keyword insertion can work wonders for your campaign. Dynamic keywords work well because they convince users that your ad was tailored specifically for their search. Whatever phrase they entered into Google Search is dynamically added to your ad's headline. If they type "Orange Garden Gnome," the top line of your ad will read "Orange Garden Gnome." Seeing the actual keywords they searched on displayed in the ad title can convince users that your business is exactly what they are looking for.

In the case of The Book Depository, on any search relating to "Books," we run the following:

[Keyword]
Free Worldwide Shipping
Big Discounts on Millions of Books
www.bookdepository.co.uk

In the case of Espressio, on any search relating to "Photo," we run the following:

[Keyword]
Create Your Photo Book
Prices from $4.99 Free P&P
www.espressio.co.uk

I use dynamic keywords, but only if my competitors are not using them. A situation can arise in which you have three or more advertisers all bidding on the same keyword and all employing dynamic keywords. The net effect for the user is a homogenization of ads—they all look the same. Ironically, it is then the ad that has the fixed text (which slightly differs from the user's choice of keywords) that becomes the ad that stands out! Try dynamic keywords but watch what your competition is doing. Remember, it's good to be different.

There are lots of ways to use *dynamic keyword insertion.* Here's a selection of examples:

- If you want the dynamic text to be all lowercase, use {keyword:Default_text}.
- If you want the dynamic text to have the first letter of the first word capitalized, use {Keyword:Default_text}.
- If you want the dynamic text to have the first letter in caps for each word, use {KeyWord:Default_text}.
- If you want the dynamic text to have the first word all in caps, use {KEYword:Default_text}.
- If you want the dynamic text to have the first word all in caps and the other words to have the first letter in caps, use {KEYWord:Default_text}.
- If you want the dynamic text to all be in caps, use {KEYWORD:Default_text}.*

* Source: http://searchengineland.com/070619-092701.php.

Personally, I use {KeyWord:Default_text} to keep the ad "clean"-looking and consistent with my static headline ads.

Remember to Include Alternative Text

Because of the character limitations of your headline (25 characters), it sometimes happens that the search term entered by the user exceeds this maximum. If this happens, your ad will display without a headline (defeating the purpose) or the headline will be truncated, which looks silly. Google allows you to volunteer *alternative text*, which will become the default text.

In the case of the dynamic The Book Depository advertisement discussed above, on any search relating to "Books," we run the following alternate text:

[Keyword: The Book Depository]
Free Worldwide Shipping
Big Discounts on Millions of Books
www.bookdepository.co.uk

Targeting Regional Traffic

Depending on the nature of your business, you may want to pay the most attention to attracting local business. Yes, the World Wide Web by nature is global, but if you're a veterinarian, you're probably going to want to attract customers within about 20 miles of your practice in Nebraska, not have anxious dog owners from London clicking through and costing you money. Within the "Target customers by location" feature, you'll notice there's a "Custom" tab. It is from there that you can drop down to the city level in terms of defining the audience you wish to attract by its geographic location. You can specify by ZIP code or city name. (I tend to set the distance parameter to 25 miles if I have a city-specific ad campaign.)

Don't forget, using regional targeting can open up new avenues for your business. If you sell large pieces of art or hefty wooden furniture, ordinarily you'll have to use couriers or even freight forwarding to get your products to your customers, wherever they are. This expensive method of getting the goods to the customer may have been incorporated into your pricing or may mean there's a substantial shipping and handling (S&H) charge added on to customer orders, but what if you could offer local customers a better deal? For anyone ordering within 25 miles, you might even be able to deliver it yourself. How does that alter your costs, and what does it mean for the customer? Regional targeting opens up lots of new opportunities, and, ironically, the World Wide Web can introduce you to a host of local people interested in your products—they just weren't aware that you are around the corner!

As a slight aside, personally, I don't think Google has quite figured out how to assure users' geographic location as accurately as it maintains, and therefore it is advised that you run a local campaign and a generic campaign. Using the veterinarian example above, I would run a city-targeted campaign for "Vet, Omaha" and a generic ad with the keywords "Vet, Omaha." Yes, it's a bit more costly, but a few weeks of data will show you which one is performing for you, if not both, and you can adapt from there.

Time Please, Gentlemen

Even if your campaign is limited to a U.S. audience and is showing only through Google Search, time can and will play a role in who clicks through on your ad and what the user then does on your site. This of course will depend on your industry, but look out for trends and patterns in when you're receiving your best CTR and best conversion rate. *Automatic bid adjustment* can be your best friend here—increasing your bid during your "peak hours," and therefore your ad's position, can be hugely beneficial. Is there a spike during lunch hour? What about first thing in the morning or toward the late afternoon, when workers' minds are no longer on the tasks they're being paid for? The information is there, so use it.

Surfing under the Influence . . .

This is only conjecture, but I have seen enough evidence to think that there are certainly sales to be made after bars kick everyone out. Take a month to prove or disprove my theory, but for a number of businesses (including wooden toys!) I've increased my bids during the hours of 10 p.m. to 1 a.m., attained a temporary higher position, and reaped the rewards of dads (and moms) coming home from a night on the town and shelling out a small fortune on a gift for Junior. The increase in the bid might be only 10 to 20 percent, which may equate to pennies, but the shopper under the influence is generous and covers the increased cost quite nicely.

6

Writing Killer Ads

Sell, Sell, Sell

We all have our own ways of writing sales messages. Within the constraints of the tight character count on AdWords, good ad writing is a fine art. Different messages and styles work for different industries, and only by testing your ads will you know what works for your business.

As an experiment, try the "three mentions" rule—that is, whatever your core keyword for this particular ad group is, be sure to mention it three times in your ad. This can be in the header and twice in the text, or you could include a mention in the display URL. However you choose to do it, try it and see what happens. It could be too much of a "hard sell" for your business, but equally, it could be the most successful ad you ever run.

Squeeze Every Single Character

Using the display URL to continue your sales message is a good tactic. There's a lot to be said for including "power" words within the URL that add to the overall message of the ad:

www.bookdespository.co.uk/freebook

www.bookdepository.co.uk/buy1get1free

If this is the angle you'd like to pursue, by all means go for it. Don't forget that if you require up to four more characters, you can always remove the "www." from the start of the display URL (see Figure 6.1).

Also don't forget that the display URL is not actually determining the destination address. Therefore, the rules of capitalization can extend to the display URL. Which of the following is going to grab your attention?

Squeezing everything in
it's hard work sometimes making
sure you can say everthing you want
shavingoffthewww.com/makesmoreroom

Figure 6.1

www.bookdepository.co.uk/freebook

or

www.BookDepository.co.uk/FreeBook

Less Is More

Contrary to the natural marketing instinct to max out the sales message within the limited word count available, I can't stress enough how important it is to play with your ad copy continually and explore all the possibilities—to see what works for your business. Toward the end of my AdWords campaign with Toytopia, there were more and more advertisers bidding on "my" keywords, and the search pages were beginning to get very busy with hard-sell ads vying for attention.

I'll admit that I didn't have much faith in the soft approach being successful, but you have to give these things a try . . . and I was pleasantly surprised. Amid all that noise on the page, users chose the most simple of the ads on offer. I deliberately chose to be in position 5, and the clicks came flooding through. This turned out to be one of my most successful ads for the keyword "Wooden Toys" (see Figure 6.2).

Try something similar; it just might work!

Wooden Toys
looking for a good home...
www.toytopia.co.uk

Figure 6.2

They Know . . .

Although you should remember to include a call to action within your ad—whether it's an attractive price point or an invitation to register—don't be tempted to include "click here." For a start, Google will not approve and the ad will be removed, but more important, it is a waste of words and an insult to your potential customers. They know to click it if they're interested; they managed to boot up their computers, launch a Web browser, and enter a keyword into Google Search to find your ad. Users know what to do next. Here are some calls to action that are allowed:

Download Our Catalogue
Browse Our Range
Free Report
Free Quotation
Apply Now
Sign Up Now
Free Demo
Free Trial

It may be a matter of personal taste, but I am not a huge fan of using the word "buy" in AdWords. I think it's pretty clear that all AdWords advertisements are promoting a service or a product that customers will have to purchase, so adding the word "buy" is somewhat superfluous and a waste of your very limited word count. Use your word count to promote the product or service by name and phrase the ad in such a way that users will want to click through and buy without having it spelled out.

Words that can be effective in your ad, depending on your business, are those relating to time—you're busy, and your potential customers are no different. "Sign up now," "Act now," "Act today," and "Limited offer" have all been used extremely effectively in a number of different campaigns for my own businesses and those of my clients.

Unless you've already built a reputation for yourself, it is inadvisable to quote your company name in the headline of an ad—it's already there in the URL, so don't waste precious words by repeating yourself. It's the sales message that will persuade users to click through to your site, not your company name or trading name.

Asking the Audience

Good ad copy piques the reader's interest. And there's no better way to get people interested in what you have to say than to ask them a question you already know the answer to.

In the case of a franchise business or an opportunity for home workers—part-time, full-time, or casual—money talks. Without using wild and ridiculous claims of instant wealth, ask away: "Want to earn $50 an hour at your computer?" That's good money whatever industry you work in . . . tell me how! If I were looking for an opportunity, I'd click on that question because the answer is almost certainly "yes." However, conversely, I wouldn't click on an ad that asked "Want to make $5,000 a day?" because unless the job involves selling copious amounts of cocaine or robbing banks, it isn't going to happen—and I'm not even going to click to find out the "secret."

Asking questions can work in any industry: "Looking for an honest real estate agent?" "Looking for pain-free dental surgery?" "Want to know all the facts about our secondhand cars?"

Instructions can work too: "Create your will in just five simple steps." "Sign up now for a homeowner's loan." Say what it is you want the users to do and call them to action.

To Price or Not to Price . . .

Adding prices to your ad can work for or against you. I have used and will continue to use ads that include prices for some products but avoid pricing altogether for other products. It depends on a number of factors, not the least whether your prices are cheaper than those of the competition, whether your competition is quoting prices, and whether the product or service you are selling is driven by price.

As with all of this advice, try it and see for yourself. Only you will know for sure whether it works for your ads, in your industry, and for your keywords.

As a rule of thumb, if my prices are far cheaper than those of the competition, I'll sing and dance about my pricing. If my prices are similar or higher, I'll push other features or benefits of my service and leave it up to the customers to decide whether they want to click through.

Being the cheapest will not always guarantee you a click-through. As consumers, we are driven by a number of factors, and quite often price is not the most important one.

Describe as Best You Can

Yes, your ad is a sales tool. As much as you want to add as many "power" words and audience grabbers as possible, your ad's primary purpose is to attract users to a specific product or service. As much as your marketing instinct is crying out for you to include "Free shipping," "No obligation quote," and "Free download," have you first conveyed what it is you do? I won't know if I want free shipping if I don't know what it is you're selling!

If your competition is hammering home power words in their ads, yours will stand out if it doesn't also do that. That gives you more room to make it absolutely clear that this ad is for this product.

Writing Tips

Everyone has a unique writing style (although my editor would argue that my writing style is not so much unique as just plain wrong) and nuances of grammar and punctuation. The good news is that these nuances can be the difference between a successful ad and a mediocre ad. When word count can translate into cash, every single comma, period, and, everyone's favorite, semicolon plays a vital role in an advertisement. Play around with punctuation the same way you do with words. I sometimes end an ad message with three dots. I'm hoping readers understand this to mean that "there's more" and click through accordingly. Although it might be correct to use a comma, use a hyphen instead, or even a dash.

- If you can be specific in your ad, do so. "Increase your efficiency by 25 percent" looks pretty impressive; I wonder if I'll click through to find out more.
- If there's an opportunity to endorse, do so—Winner WhatCar 2009—but only if it's true!
- The words "new," "improved," and "free" tend to be crowd-pleasers, but only if they're true and relevant—you may fool users into clicking through, but if they're not buying from you, you're just wasting your money.
- It won't stop everyone from clicking through, but if it's applicable, say: "For

women only," "Only for men," or "Over 18s only."

- If you're concerned about space, it's acceptable to use an ampersand (&) instead of "and"—that's two more characters for you to play with.

Again, these tips have been generated through trial and error over a number of years of AdWords campaigns. Without doubt, though, it is important to capitalize every word in your ad (except for "in," "on," "and," etc.).

So, regardless of your headline, an ad saying the following:

Great selection, fast service, and free shipping worldwide

becomes:

Great Selection—Fast Service
Free Shipping Worldwide

The second version is far more eye-catching and more likely to get you that click-through.

Never before have spelling and grammar been so important. Yes, there is some room for maneuvering in terms of using "&" instead of "and" and experimenting with a dash instead of a comma or semicolon, but there is absolutely no room for error in terms of spelling and knowing when to use the plural form or an apostrophe. There are some shocking ads on display with errors that will make you wince. Admittedly, some people must be clicking on them—otherwise they wouldn't last long—but how much more effective would they be if the ad writer knew when to use the word "babies" instead of "baby's," for instance?

I write for a living, but I still make mistakes—we all do—so I have an editor. The same should be true for you and your ads. Have someone check them over for glaring errors. It's not an admission of failure or incompetence; it's common sense. Your business is at stake, and if you're really embarrassed about it, you could always just ask for the proofreader's opinion about which ad he or she thinks is going to be more successful—having read through the selection, he or she will hedge the bet and point out ever so politely that you've mixed your "their" with your "there" . . . again.

Finally, be sure to target your audience with the language it wants to read. Quite simply, if you're trying to attract consumers, tailor your ad to them; if you're trying to attract businesses, the copy must be different. Consumers generally buy just one of anything, whereas businesses often buy in bulk. You can deter the wrong sort of user or appeal to the right sort simply by including the quantities you sell in the ad. The phrase "free delivery on bulk orders" tells me you're selling to the trade no matter what the product is or what else you've written in the ad. Then, if I'm a business, I might click through; if I'm buying for myself, I won't.

After the Click-Through, What Then?

Although you can tweak and alter your ad copy until it's nearly perfect and enjoy click-through rates that would make your competitors weep (if they knew), it all adds up to absolutely nothing if you don't convert those click-through prospects into paying customers. Conversion is king, and the only way you're going to convert users into consumers is by making sure the destination URL is optimized not only to receive potential customers but also to keep them there and make their path to purchase as seamless and painless as possible.

Optimize the Language of Your Destination URL

Language is a beautiful thing. We have dictionaries full of words to choose from, and we have always been told to take our time explaining things to others in using the written word. Then along came the information superhighway to add to our already busy, no-time-to-stop lifestyles. Net result—Web language was born.

Web language is short, informal, and at times quite chatty, but this does not mean that the basic rules of grammar and spelling are any less important—it just means that you can bend the rules occasionally. There is no excuse for mistakes, but you can be clever with your copy, and users will be extremely forgiving (and grateful) if you can include a bit of humor in your Web pages.

Sound Bites

No matter how well crafted each word of text on a Web page is, only a small percentage of the page actually will be read. We, the users, will scan quickly, hoping that our eye catches something related to what it is that drove us to the page in the first place. It has to be very well written copy indeed to first gain our attention and then make us change our instinct from moving on to reading on.

Keep your text short, snappy, and focused. Make reference to the keywords you used to entice users to click on your ad—if all the references to what's brought them this far peter out, they'll abandon your site.

Observe your competitors' sites shamelessly. Are they doing something that is different or doing something that is better? If they are funny, make your text funnier. If their sites are a little tongue-in-cheek, compete with wit and take the war of words to them.

Stop Jabbering

As a rule of thumb, try not to use more than three paragraphs to describe a product or service. Paraphrasing the old maxim about presentations, tell them what it is, tell them again, and then remind them what they've just read. Be economical with your words but reinforce the keywords that will help you sell. By all means allow users to find out more, such as technical specifications, testimonials, and related products, but don't let this get in the way of the synopsis. Offer this additional information in the form of links to other pages on your site. Users like to know that there is more information available if they wish to follow the links, but often just that knowledge acts as a substitute for actually reading it. The trick is to have information at hand but for it not to be fighting for space with the sound bite.

Don't be shy about what you have to offer—you've enticed the users to click through to this specific page; now work on them. Be proud, be daring, and show them a bit of cleavage to whet their appetites. Bearing in mind that you have only about 10 seconds to hook a user, make it good.

Up and to the Front

No matter how much or how little content you have on the destination URL, the key to using space effectively is to *push it up and to the front*. The simple rule is to push the most appealing or important products or articles to the top of the page, with everything else forming a frame. This should, of course, be the product or service around which your AdWords ad was tailored. These words or images or products are your best assets—your family jewels—and must be promoted and supported. Bearing in mind that most users will not scroll to the bottom of the page—ever—what is above the fold (and therefore will be seen the most) must entice, tease, and fulfill your visitors' curiosity enough for them to read on or make a purchase.

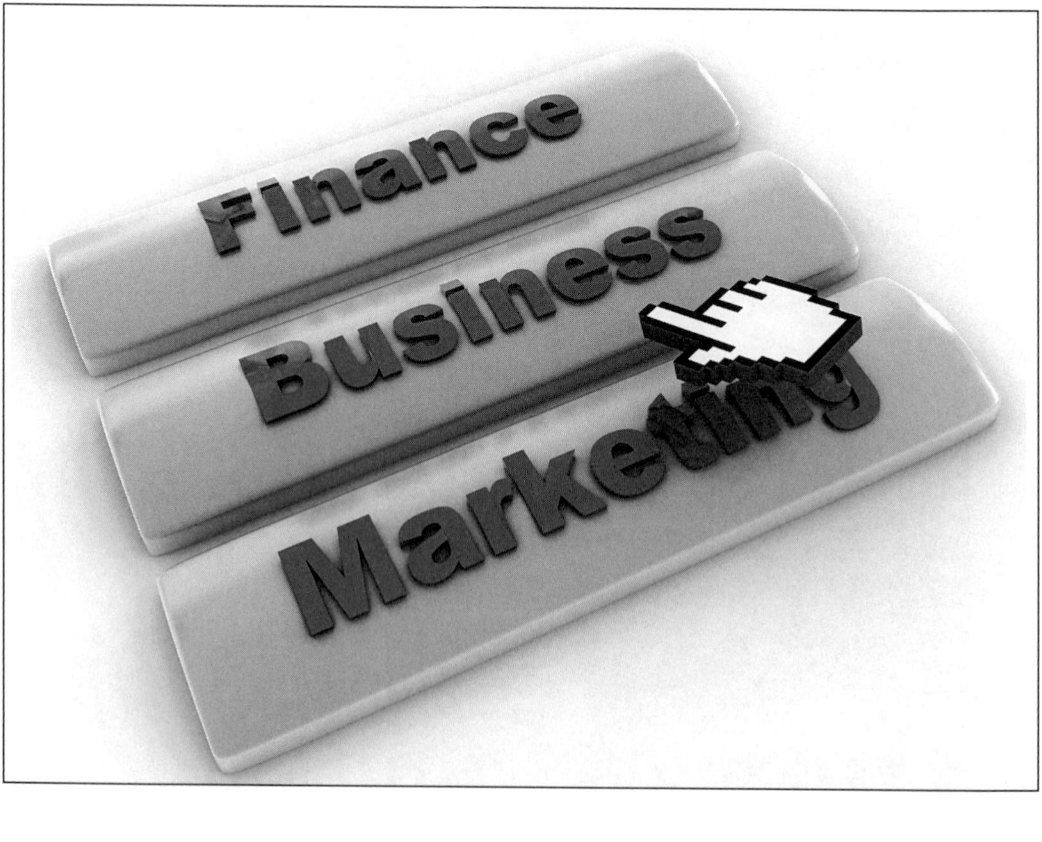
Finance
Business
Marketing

7
Ad Testing, Tracking, and Converting

Taking Stock

You've established a campaign, and it's been running for at least a couple of months. You've got real data to work from, and you also have a better feel for what AdWords are and what they can do for your business. Every eight weeks or so, I'd advise running a sort of campaign health check. Here's what you should review.

Automatically Optimizing Ad Serving

This is a superb feature except, of course, if you are testing new or altered ads. Google allows you to rotate ads evenly to split test one against another. It also offers to optimize your ads automatically by serving up your best-performing ads more frequently. However, when you're testing a number of ads and want to identify the best performer, you must turn off the automatic ad optimizer to ensure that each version of the ad is displayed evenly. Otherwise, the ad that first shows promise is optimized and shown more often, which means the exercise becomes self-fulfilling and you'll never know the true strength of the other n versions. . . .

Naming Convention

When you start your first AdWords ad, it's difficult to know where you are going next and how many ad groups you're going to end up with. Personally, I always call the first campaign "Campaign number 1"—not original, not very exciting, but it works. Now that you've got a number of ads running, it's a good time to start using a convention. Be logical, because one day you're going to want to go on vacation and will have to leave your account in the hands of someone else (aargh!!). Will that person be able to understand the ads? No, I didn't think so. Name your babies with care!

Settings

Often, when first creating an AdWords campaign, we leave most of the default settings as they are in a rush to get the ad out there and working. But the defaults don't work for everyone, especially in terms of distribution options, language, country, and region. Do you still find that the ads served on Google's Search Network and Content Network are working for you? (Did you even know you were signed up for them?) Review them and make a decision to drop or keep them. Similarly, is it time to add or delete countries and/or regions? If there's dead wood, chop it out. If you've conquered the United States, move on to Europe or Asia provided that they're applicable to your product or service.

Keyword Refreshment

Maybe your ads are working well with the keywords you've chosen, but remember to use this review time to see what's hot and what's not—there may well have been a huge shift in user behavior. Keep abreast and make changes if necessary.

Success?

In a nutshell, are you getting a return on your investment? How much are you spending a month on AdWords, and what does that equate to in sales? Is that figure acceptable, too low, or beyond your wildest dreams? It's unlikely to be beyond your wildest dreams no matter how well it's performing, so what are you going to do to improve things? That's right: tweak, edit, rewrite, and launch another campaign.

If No Sale, What?

Sometimes, especially in the early days of a new venture or when an established company diversifies into a new product line or service, sales aren't the only indicator of whether an AdWords campaign is working for you. What is important to measure is the action your AdWords ad caused. Did the ad bring users to a form that needed completing? If so, was it completed? Did the ad bring users to a page that in turn had links to other pages on the site or other sites? If so, how many of those links were clicked? What did the user do next? Obviously, only some of this information is collected by Google AdWords, so you'll need as much visibility as possible in terms of what users are doing on your site too. If this is something that's currently lacking, you need to look into it quickly.

Testing Protocol

It's very tempting to make huge alterations to your ads, especially if their perform-ance has been somewhat lackluster. Don't do it. Make only one alteration at a time and then retest. This can be a simple alteration in the sentence syntax or a change in wording. Retest, and if it's still not working, make another alteration.

Though I've done this for quite a few years, I am still amazed at how much more successful an ad can be if I just alter a word or change the structure of the message. If you make blanket alterations—essentially creating a brand-new ad rather than modifying the one you already have—you'll miss out on the hidden gems you've already created and be forever making alterations without seeing the benefit.

Play with Price

AdWords is a constantly changing marketplace—new advertisers join in, and old hands give up or lose interest. Hear this: AdWords punishes the complacent and re-wards those who embrace change.

Even if an ad is working, don't stop testing variations—and not only how the ad looks, feels, and reads. Also alter the bid price and monitor the effect this has on your CTR. You may notice that your CTR goes down in a direct relationship to a lower bid, but, equally, as a result of a number of variables, you may notice that the ad actually performs better yet is costing you less money. How cool is that!?

Whether your CTR goes up or down, your constant experimenting is feeding valuable data into your campaign. Before long you'll know exactly what works for your business in your industry.

What about Conversion?

If you talk to advertisers who use AdWords day in and day out, you sometimes can get sucked in to their way of thinking—namely, that CTR is the be-all and end-all. But it's not. It's only half the battle.

Having a great CTR is marvelous, but is it making you money? More important, have you got the tools in place to measure this? Google's suite of tools in relation to AdWords is impressive, and most of the data you need are available at the click of a mouse through one dashboard, but please don't forget to use (or if you haven't got anything set up, make sure to do that) your own stats and user logs and any back-end facilities you have to monitor traffic behavior on your Web pages. What are users doing once they've clicked through to your destination URL? If it's a generic ad pointing to your home page, are they navigating through the site or are they bouncing (leaving the home page without delving further into the site)? If you are pointing to a specific page such as a registration form or a product detail page, are users completing the form or placing the item in their shopping basket, abandoning the site, or navigating somewhere else? You have to know the answers to these questions to know whether your AdWords campaign is effective.

Set your Web site targets the same way you would with any resource. If users are navigating away from the destination URL, there is something wrong with the page or the message you're using to draw them in. If users are hitting your home page and then bouncing, the reality of your site hasn't delivered what the ad promised. Fix these problems.

CTR is important, but not if the click-throughs aren't becoming paying customers.

Revise Negative Keywords and Improve Your CTR

No matter how well you research your keywords and even your list of negative keywords before the campaign, you still will be attracting unwanted clicks. It is only with the data you start receiving that you can see for yourself whether your lists are working. Chances are, when you investigate the raw query strings, you'll notice that there are lots of click-throughs from a certain keyword that isn't converting—add that problem keyword to your negative list.

Be sure to consider whether you want to block these new negative keywords across your entire account or add them to specific ad groups.

Testing Your Ads

Split testing your ads is often a long (well, actually, it's never-ending) and somewhat tricky task, but it is the time you spend testing your ads against one another that ultimately will turn a mediocre AdWords experience into a killer campaign. It is the small subtleties of changing a word in the copy here and adding a negative keyword there that can improve the CTR of an ad by an entire percentage point, sometimes even more.

Split testing is the art of having very similar ads competing against one another for the same keywords. All the parameters are the same—the target geographic locations, the price you are bidding, the keywords, and, of course, the negative keywords. The difference is in the ad copy—a subtle textual difference that could be one word or even just the order in which the words are displayed. The result you are looking for ordinarily is an increase in the CTR, proof that one ad attracts more users than another.

To initialize a split test, click on "Create New Ad" and start writing. There is a school of thought that says it's wise to test a number of ad variants simultaneously—the argument is that you'll find your killer ad more quickly with, say, four versions competing against one another. This may work for you, but I think this process is called A/B testing for a reason—it's A versus B, and once ad B (or A) proves to be the definite winner, you replace the loser with another slightly tweaked ad and the process starts again.

The two (or more) ads you choose to be A/B will not be shown at *exactly* the same rate. However, it's pretty much a 50-50 split, and once you have about seven days' worth of data, you'll begin to see from the results that one ad is outperforming the other. Now, most of the time the improved performance of one ad over another amounts to merely one-tenth of a percent. But that is still an improvement, and if you can manage to increase your CTR even by one-tenth of a percent every test cycle, you're going to get more click-throughs and, presumably, more customers.

When you do split testing, you also should be looking at the bigger picture—although improving CTR is incredibly important (not the least because it means your ad is not disabled and lives another day), you also should use split testing to measure any changes in your *conversion ratio* (the number of users who become consumers) and ultimately your ROI. Although there are numerous factors that will determine whether someone clicking through on your ad ends up buying a product or service from you, it all starts with that click-through and attracting the right user in the first place.

When you are writing new copy for the competing "B" ad, don't be tempted to change too much—subtlety is the name of the game. Week 1 could entail adding a call to action, week 2 could involve modifying the display URL. Too many alterations and you're not A/B testing anymore; you're trying to compare apples with oranges, and though the "B" ad might do very well, you still won't know whether you can improve the "A" ad and the exercise is wasted.

So Much Testing, So Little Time . . .

Testing new ads, altering copy, split testing "A" and "B" ads—it all takes time. I would argue that it's time well spent, but it may be too much for you to handle on your own, especially if you run a small operation and your time and expertise are expected and needed elsewhere. Personally, I love to stay in control of my AdWords campaigns so that I can react immediately and retire ads that are failing and boost ads that are doing well. But we all have lives outside of marketing, and even hardworking folks such as yourselves deserve to take a holiday once in a while rather than melting under the constant weight of the responsibility required to stay ahead of the game.

Help is at hand and is available for what is a nominal fee compared with what a medium-size or large AdWords campaign might be costing you per month. For around $20 a month, there are companies that will take the pain out of testing. Here are two of them:

www.loweryourbidprice.com
http://www.winneralert.com/

Pay their fees and sit back and wait for the e-mail notifications to come through. All the hard work has been done, and your "winning" ads will be highlighted so that you can get on with the next test.

It's worth visiting the Winner Alert home page just to read the sales pitch, which is refreshingly funny. Added to that, they give you a free 14-day trial.

Measuring Conversion

There is a good reason why Google gives you a chance to enter a destination URL and a display URL, and if you find you're entering the same information into both fields, chances are that you are not exploiting your AdWords campaign to its maximum potential. Although the display URL should be clear, concise, and clutter-free (even if you decide to use it as an opportunity to include a sales message or "power word"), the destination URL can be anything you like, and the emphasis here is on finding a way to *use* it to help you track conversion. Figure 7.1 shows what I mean.

All I have done here is embed a simple code into the URL so that when the user clicks through to my Web site—in this case my home page—I can track his or her actions through my own back-end software. In this example, the user's visit to my site tells me that he or she clicked on an ad from my "template" keyword group and it was ad variant number 53. Without this code, I wouldn't have a clue which ad had drawn the user to my home page. Although I would know the referrer was Google AdWords, I wouldn't be able to discern which ad had earned me money.

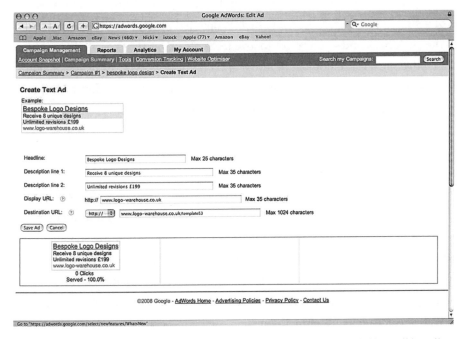

Figure 7.1 By adding "template53" to the destination URL, I can track what users clicking on this particular ad get up to on my Web site.

By copying this technique across the entire range of ad groups and with the help of a simple Excel spreadsheet (which is updated automatically by a data feed from the site's back end—you've got to love technology!), I receive a daily report on how effective my ads are not just in terms of CTR but also in terms of conversion— and I can put a financial value on that conversion and decide whether to suspend, edit, or even increase my spend on a particular ad or ad group.

Knowing What to Measure

When you're embarking on your Google AdWords campaign, your primary goal is, of course, to achieve a healthy CTR. It is this click-through rate that ultimately will decide whether Google will allow your ad to continue or whether the ad will be disabled. It is also the click-through rate that measures how effective your ad is with the general search public; ultimately, if people are clicking on your ad, you're doing something right—whether they then become customers depends on how good a job your Web site does in converting them.

Remember, though, that CTR is not everything. Yes, it will remain in the background as a critical yardstick to measure performance, but as you embark on your Google AdWords experience, it is paramount that you and the other stakeholders in your business know exactly what you wish to achieve with Google AdWords. If your main goal is to drive traffic from Google or its partners to your site—where, ultimately, the user will buy at least one product or service from you there and then—that's great and relatively straightforward. It also could be that you want to use Google AdWords to promote a certain aspect of your business, such as one of the many services you offer or a certain product range (whether low- or high-value) that you feel will benefit from online advertising. In addition, most businesses, although they want instant sales, should be using Google AdWords for a number of other reasons too. Brand awareness is still an important part of the marketing mix, and AdWords can help you achieve this. Bringing down the cost per acquisition, compared with traditional or offline marketing efforts, is another important aspect of the marketing mix.

Whatever your goals, do not lose sight of them. Utilizing Google AdWords is hard work; it is time-consuming, and there are no shortcuts or viable ways to avoid having to do the research or the constant monitoring. However, when AdWords works, it works well, and it's easy to get caught up in the excitement of a successful campaign—but how do you measure success? Is it CTR? Is it ROI? Is it brand awareness and company exposure? Is it cost of new customer acquisition? I think it's all of these things combined, and that means you need to be looking at all of these measurables closely.

From User to Consumer: The Customer's Journey

In Chapter 6 we looked at the importance of great ad copy that leads to a high click-through rate, which in turn leads users to your destination URL. But to convert, your users must do more than read copy on your Web site; they must interact—ideally, that interaction means calling you, completing a form, or ordering a product. How easy is that process on your site?

Successful businesses on the Internet are not made just by driving thousands or millions of people to your site—if you have a strong enough offering or buckets of cash to spend on AdWords, that is relatively easy. The trick is to convert your users into consumers and ensure that when they leave, some of their money has been left with you. . . .

Your site is not there to look pretty; it's there for a reason—to make money. Unashamedly pimp your site and don't let your working pages go to sleep on the job, so to speak. Keep tweaking your Web pages; keep improving your offering.

The Road to Damascus

A great way to understand why not every visitor ends up buying products or downloading information from your site is to focus on how you behave when surfing the Internet. Not every single user on your Web site will consume—and there is nothing you can do about that. But with the average conversion ratio of anything between 1 and 5 percent, how can you ensure that you are at the top rather than the bottom of this scale (or even on it)? First, there are going to be visitors to your site who really are *just looking* for whatever reason—your ad made them aware of your existence. Second, there are visitors who found you by complete accident and don't know where they are going or why they are there—they simply saw your ad and loved the message so much that they clicked. Some will scan your destination URL and leave immediately (bouncers), whereas others will have a quick read because something in the ad caught their eye but won't become consumers. When you visit a Web site, what dictates whether you end up buying? Well, a number of factors come into play. . . .

Big Brand, Little Brand

Brand awareness will happen over time through trust (maybe of a parent company or from sympathetic PR) or because it is bought through a massive advertising campaign with a budget that would leave most of us aghast. Branding does take time, but once your brand is established, it will help users become consumers just because of who you are. Everything might be right about your site—the look, the feel, the navigation, and the price of your products or services—but Jo Bloggs hasn't heard of you before and, certainly when you are selling products that cost more than about $25, becomes reluctant to part with his cash for no better reason than that you're not familiar enough . . . yet.

Giving It Up

A major complaint from users, when they are not chasing their orders, refers to a lack of information available on Web sites. Now, although it is important to keep Web copy short, snappy, and to a minimum, there is no excuse for not including the basic information about the products you are expecting your users to spend money on. If your ad has attracted users to click through, their experience on your site must be perfect. Users want more information—about the product, about the service, about the meaning of life. If you don't provide the information necessary to make users comfortable enough to purchase, they'll be off to another site where the information is more freely available. Net result: lost business and lost revenue. And all because you have not repeated verbatim what has been provided to you by the manufacturer or supplier or your own sales documentation . . . very poor indeed.

Where Exactly Am I?

Users will feel a lot happier about spending time on your site and committing to spending some money if they can get around the site in a logical manner. It's paramount to ensure that you have good navigation, with links and buttons that not only work but also take users quickly and seamlessly exactly where they want to go. Improve your site navigation and you will see a rise in your conversion ratio.

Your destination URL works, but once users continue on their journey within your site and embark along the order pipeline, the pages have to maintain the quality and integrity they have already come to expect.

The Order Pipeline

The buying process itself can scare a lot of users away even though until that moment you had them hooked on you, your pricing, and your products. It defies belief that Web sites spend all their time and effort (and, it would appear, cash) on designing the ultimate site in terms of attractive navigation and well-presented products but then let themselves down spectacularly with the final and most important step—the shopping basket and order pipeline. As much time and effort should go into the design and implementation of the order pipeline as went into the look and feel of the home page. Getting users to select products or services from your site and put them into a basket or cart is only half the battle—you now need to get them to walk through the checkout without abandoning the purchase.

Despite the best efforts of your AdWords campaign to attract new visitors to the site, the efforts of merchandising to ensure that the right products are available at the right price, and the efforts of the sales/editorial department to present the products in the best possible light, if it all goes wrong at the end and users find it difficult to buy from you, it is all in vain. Make the ordering process problem-free for the customers and don't let them leave without spending some money!

The process of users placing items into their shopping baskets and their subsequent path to purchase often is referred to as the order pipeline. This is the distance and the number of pages consumers must face before their chosen purchases become their own. Just as good Web design is all about offering both simplicity and usability, an effective order pipeline is short and to the point. If you had to complete an obstacle course every time you wanted to do your weekly grocery shopping, you soon would look to another supermarket that was far easier to navigate and give it your business. The same is true for Web sites.

Just the Basics, Please

When you are designing or redesigning your order pipeline, look to shave off as many stages as possible between a user selecting what he or she wants to buy and the order confirmation page. You need to look at your current setup and define what details are important for this order and what can be captured at a later date. If you have the time and the tools, look at how many customers place an item in their baskets and how many complete their orders. The lost business is absolutely heartbreaking. You will be losing about 50 percent of your business for every page of the order pipeline. Thus, if 100 people put an item into their baskets and there are five pages of order pipeline, you will be looking at just over three orders actually being completed. Imagine the difference if you take away two of those pages—you will be enjoying over 12 orders per 100 instead of just three.

Keep Them Informed

Even after your order pipeline has been perfected, there are some delays that you simply cannot eradicate, and the main delay occurs when the Web site is trying to confirm with your bank that the customer's card details are legitimate. Although you cannot speed up this process, you can let your customers know what is going on. Even if it is as simple as showing a sand timer or a message, make it clear that the site is still working and it's just looking for information from another source.

Similarly, it is probably worth your while to offer a phone number and a fax number for people who want to leave their credit card details. Although most Web users no longer worry about the safety of their card details, there still are users who feel safer reading their card numbers to a human being rather than entering the details online. You are within your rights to charge a surcharge to cover the associated administrative costs. Having someone staff the phones for users who are having difficulty ordering from you most certainly will give you a good ROI; letting your users abandon their baskets will not.

One Eye on the Future

Sadly, at the time of this writing, the technology is only in beta form, but from what I can gather, "click to play" video advertising is coming . . . and it has *so* many possibilities. Video advertising (currently available only through Google's Content Network) is going to make AdWords truly Web 2.0—that is, it will allow the displaying of information, on demand, in a truly multimedia way. AdWords still will be displayed as text-only ads, but there will be an option (and it will be very much opt-in to keep within the principles of Google's "less is more" business ethic) to see video ads alongside, or as well as, the text ad. Imagine the possibilities—a 20-second movie-style "trailer" showing your product in action or walking users through the registration process.

Why will it work? Well, we already see that Google's acquisition of YouTube in 2006 is generating a new form of text-based advertising that will appear on a mutually relevant piece of YouTube content. But what about search-based TV commercial–quality video advertising content that is *pulled* onto a potential customer's screen, based on a product or relevant service search query? Let's first look quickly at what's wrong with traditional TV commercial advertising to give you an idea of where AdWords could be headed. For starters, advertisers can't be sure who is watching their advertisements. TV commercial creation and broadcast costs are prohibitive to all but a few major brands. The ad is *pushed* onto the screen and not requested by the viewer. There are now so many TV channels to choose from, fragmenting an already shrinking viewing audience. There is no way to prove the financial success of your television advertising campaign with any accuracy—and, of course, there now exists hardware that allows the viewer to "skip" the advertising altogether. Not as compelling a marketing tool as it once seemed, then.

Traditional TV advertising's loss, however, is to become AdWords' gain. The AdWords system of advertisement delivery solves all these problems, so if you could combine the instant audiovisual impact of a TV campaign with the ruthless efficiency of AdWords, you would have a highly effective business development tool at your disposal. A fantastic new era is emerging in which all AdWords advertisers will be able to run their own highly affordable, professionally created TV commercials through an AdWords account.

The potential is massive, and at the moment there seems to be only one serious service provider in the United States ready to harness this new dawn of video PPC marketing: www.admoogle.tv/.

Take a look and use it if it appeals to you. And don't forget to quote "Jon's AdWords Book"—who knows, they might even find it in their heart to give me a commission!

A Word of Warning . . .

If you've created a campaign and it's working really well for you, that's great. I'm all for a bit of backslapping. In fact, when working for U.S. companies, I've even been known to join in with the occasional "whoop" every now and again. Yes, success is great, but don't rest on your laurels, not even for a week. AdWords campaigns work—you've seen that by now with your own eyes in relation to your own site—but there are always competitors waiting to leap into your position. Rest assured that as more and more users become familiar with AdWords and realize the importance of testing, measuring, and tweaking, they'll be nipping at your ankles from now on.

Stay ahead of the game. Continue to test, continue to run new ads, and constantly strive to improve your ROI. You can never refine too much. Yes, you'll take some wrong turns along the way, but you'll know how to revert to your successful form again.

Survivors adapt; those who remain static perish.

Good luck!

Index

Notes

Notes

Notes